Final Justice
at Adobe
Wells

Crossway Books by
STEPHEN BLY

THE STUART BRANNON WESTERN SERIES
Hard Winter at Broken Arrow Crossing
False Claims at the Little Stephen Mine
Last Hanging at Paradise Meadow
Standoff at Sunrise Creek
Final Justice at Adobe Wells

THE NATHAN T. RIGGINS WESTERN ADVENTURE SERIES (AGES 9–14)
The Dog Who Would Not Smile
Coyote True
You Can Always Trust a Spotted Horse
The Last Stubborn Buffalo in Nevada

Final Justice at Adobe Wells

Stephen Bly

CROSSWAY BOOKS • WHEATON, ILLINOIS
A DIVISION OF GOOD NEWS PUBLISHERS

Final Justice at Adobe Wells

Copyright © 1993 by Stephen Bly.

Published by Crossway Books, a division of Good News Publishers, 1300 Crescent Street, Wheaton, Illinois 60187.

Cover illustration: Den Schofield

First printing, 1993

Printed in the United States of America

Library of Congress Cataloging-in-Publication Data
Bly, Stephen A., 1944-
    Final Justice at Adobe Wells / Stephen Bly.
        p.   cm. — (The Stuart Brannon western adventure series)
    I. Title.   II. Series: Bly, Stephen A., 1944-   Stuart Brannon
western adventure series.
PS3552.L93F56 1993   813'.54—dc20   93-14185
ISBN 0-89107-744-8

01	00	99	98	97	96	95	94	93
15	14	13	12	11	10	9	8	7	6	5	4	3	2	1

For a list of other books by
Stephen Bly
or information regarding speaking engagements
write:
Stephen Bly
Winchester, Idaho 83555

For
*L*ILA *B*ISHOP
who rode
with me down
many a dusty
editorial
trail

O N E

"Mr. Brannon, I feel like I've know'd you for years, what with all them stories about ya in the books and papers and all!"

Stuart Brannon didn't bother sitting up, but continued to recline, glancing with one eye at the speaker.

"The way you handled them Reynoso brothers."

"Rutherford."

"Yep, them's the ones. I read in Hawthorne Miller how you had all seven of them cornered at one time and—"

"There were only three of them."

"But they was the biggest, baddest gang in Wyoming!"

"Colorado and New Mexico."

"Yep. I know'd that. That there Hawthorne Miller is a fine writer. A mighty fine writer, yes, sir. Why, one of my very favorites is the one about how you stopped Slippery Ed Bennett up in Boise City."

"I've never been to Boise City."

"Like I said, I feel like I know'd ya like a brother."

"Have we met?" Brannon's dusty, broad-brimmed, black hat pulled low over his eyes blocked the sun glaring through the rail car window.

"No, sir, we ain't never met. No, sir. But it's my pleasure . . . indeed it is. Mind if I sit here?"

Without waiting for an answer, the small man with the gleaming new holster-gun belted to his hip sat down next to Brannon.

"Folks just call me Read Reynolds." He stuck out a soft hand with dirty fingernails.

"Well, Mr. Reynolds, if I'm not—"

"Read. Call me Read."

"Well, Read," Brannon pushed his hat back, eyes now boldly studying the man, "if I'm not too sociable, please excuse me. It's been a long trip and I'm nearly worn out from bouncing on stages and trains."

"Yes, sir, I imagine it has. I hear you been back in Washington tellin' them senators a thing or two."

"How'd you hear about that?" Brannon tried to scrunch back down in the seat.

"I'll tell you how, yes, sir, I will. Listen to this." A newspaper rustled in Brannon's face.

"Here it is, right here. Page 1 of the *Fort Smith Daily Record*. 'Mr. Stuart Brannon, famed gunman of the Great Southwest and recent victor in the Yavapai County War in Arizona Territory, completed his testimony yesterday before the United States Senate Committee reviewing the government's policy of settling land grant claims still unresolved from the Mexican War. Mr. Brannon insisted the government act quickly to process legitimate claims before more undue hardship and violence erupt.'"

"And here I quote Mr. Stuart Brannon himself. 'Brannon stated, "There are legitimate claims, and those folks need clear title to their property immediately. All the others should be dismissed, tried, or shot."' End of quote."

"I never said anything about shooting people."

With only a slight pause, Reynolds began again, "Here's another . . . from the *Fort Worth Daily Leader*. 'The President of the United States interrupted his short vacation to return to the White House and meet with Arizona rancher and shootist, Stuart Brannon. Insiders speculate that the President asked the now-famous gunman to be U.S. Marshal in charge of the whole Territory.'"

Brannon knew what the next question would be.

"W-well, sir," Reynolds stammered, "did he . . . you know, ask you?"

"Yep."

"What did you tell him?"

"Nope."

"Why?"

"It's too dangerous."

Reynolds sat straight up.

"It's what?" Then suddenly he slumped back down. "You're just stretchin' me, ain't ya? Probably it was just too tame—paperwork and office jobs and the like, I suppose. Yes, sir, it wouldn't be right for a man of your skill to be pushin' no pencil."

Brannon poked his head out from under his hat and stared at Reynolds.

"Read, where do you hail from?"

"South Carolina. And you?"

"Eh, Texas. How long have you been out West?"

"About two weeks now, I'd guess."

"Well, Read, just don't believe everything about the West that you read in those eastern books and papers."

"No, sir, I won't. Now listen to this—and it comes from the *New York City Observer*, so you know it's true. 'Mr. Stuart Brannon, legendary hero of Hawthorne Miller's novels, arrived in this city yesterday and single-handedly disarmed two ruffians who accosted him just outside the train depot. In a daring daylight display of. . . .'"

Read Reynolds continued to review the clippings, but Brannon had stopped listening. He thought he heard a shout from the vicinity of the dining car to the rear and definitely could feel the train beginning to slow. Reaching to the floor, he pulled a small blanket up over his shoulders, covering his waist and chest.

A lady's scream, several shouts, and a gunshot sent Read Reynolds right up out of his seat and then to the floorboards. But Brannon didn't flinch.

"Now, folks, that shot was through the ceiling. The next one will be straight into the heart of the first fool that goes for his gun!" a man shouted. "Faro's at the back with a shotgun, and Scully's totin' a satchel. We just expect you to toss in your pokes and purses nice and peaceful."

In the noise and confusion, Brannon had difficulty locating each of the three outlaws by sound alone.

"When he gets to our row, you stand up in the aisle," he growled under his breath to Reynolds.

"What? Stand? Sure."

There was a scuffle, a gasp, a slap. Then the sound of boot heels and jingling spurs.

"Well, if it ain't a brand new Colt. Put it in the bag, or you'll never see your mama again," a man's voice threatened.

"I'll have to stand to take it off," Reynolds whimpered.

"Then stand! And your friend there—roust him out. Or is he tryin' to hide under that blanket?"

"I wouldn't bother him if I were you," Reynolds cautioned as he stood to unbuckle his gun belt.

No . . . no, don't say it, Reynolds. Don't tell them who I am.

"And why not?" the man with the gun demanded.

"'Cause that's none other than Mr. Stuart Brannon and—"

At the mention of his name, Brannon heard the revolver's hammer click back as the outlaw started to fire. The responding blast from Brannon's .45 tore through the blanket and slammed into Scully's chest, causing his gun to discharge into the seat cushion as he collapsed in the aisle.

Passengers screamed and dove for protection. Brannon instantly fired a second shot at Faro at the rear of the car who had just raised the shotgun to his shoulder. The bullet caught the man at the base of the neck and tumbled him onto his back. The blast from the shotgun opened a two-foot hole in the ceiling of the Pullman car.

At the same moment the gunman at the front of the car fired at the only man standing. Read Reynolds staggered and then tumbled down into the aisle.

The jolt of the rapidly slowing train caused the remaining outlaw to stumble back against the train car door. It was just enough time for Brannon to take aim and shout, "Drop it or I shoot!"

The outlaw didn't.

Brannon did.

Babies cried.

Women screamed.

Men hollered.

And the train shuddered to a halt.

For thirty confusing minutes the westbound Southern Pacific sat forty-six miles southeast of Tucson as two dead gunmen and two wounded men were transferred to the baggage car. Stuart Brannon, Dr. Devin Dalemead, and train agent Norman Gravette rode with the wounded.

"Mr. Brannon," Gravette began, "I do hope you understand that Southern Pacific policy is to try to prevent situations like this from occurring. It's very difficult to build customers' confidence, what with you starting the shooting and—"

"Mr. Gravette," Brannon snapped, "when a man begins to pull the trigger on a loaded weapon pointed at me from only a few feet away, I intend to stop him."

"Yes, well, I understand," Gravette mumbled. "What I mean to say is, perhaps you'd be happier with some other mode of transportation."

"Are you kicking me off the railroad?"

"Heavens, no. I merely . . . I mean . . . well, I did jump the wire and sent a message about the shooting on ahead to the sheriff in Tucson."

"That ought to bring a crowd out."

"To see the famous Stuart Brannon?"

"Not hardly. But they'll be there to see these bodies. Dead out-laws always bring a crowd."

Dr. Dalemead interrupted, "Brannon, your friend Reynolds wants to talk to you."

"How does it look?"

"Nasty, but survivable."

"And the other one?"

"He'll live to spend many a day in Yuma."

"Who is he?"

"Says his name is Miles Matee, head of the Matee gang. Ever heard of him?"

"Nope."

Brannon walked over to the blanketed Reynolds. "Well, Read, we stopped them, didn't we?"

A slight smile came to the man's pale face. "Yes, sir, I believe we did. Do you think this will get written up in one of those books?"

"I doubt it."

"Surely the newspaper will make mention of it. You'll tell the paper, won't ya?"

"I tell you what, Reynolds. I won't tell the newspaper any-thing. I'll leave that up to you."

"Ya will? You mean they'll want to talk to me?"

"I reckon so. But tell them the truth, Read. No stretchers."

"No, sir, no stretchers. Just the truth."

"Doc says you'll pull through just fine."

"Only problem is, he says I can't go nowhere fer two weeks."

"Tucson's a nice town. You'll enjoy the stay."

"Well, now, that ain't the point. Ya see, I've got to get down to Mexico—to a place called Adobe Wells."

"What's so important?"

"I got a letter to deliver all the way from South Carolina. And I'm suppose to meet a man within the week."

"Gettin' shot up is a fairly good excuse for being a little late."

"Look, I can't be late with this. It's my solemn duty."

"Duty to whom?"

"It's a personal matter. I've just got to get there."

"Where's this Adobe Wells?"

"Somewhere northeast of Magdalena, close to the Sierra Madres. It can't be all that hard to find."

"Have you ever been to Mexico?"

"No, sir, Mr. Brannon, I ain't. But I got these friends down there, and I need to get the letter to them."

"Reynolds, you aren't carrying a bunch of those phony land grant papers, are you?"

"Oh, no, sir. Well, actually, I guess I don't rightly know what's in the letter. It's all sealed up tight, and my instructions were not to open it. I was to deliver it to Rube Woolsey at Adobe Wells, and he would give me a letter to take back to South Carolina."

"So you're just playing like the pony express?"

"Yes, sir, I suppose I am. But it did give me a chance to see the wild West."

"Was it as wild as you figured?"

"Yep. Wait until I tell them back home that I teamed up with Stuart Brannon. We did team up on that deal, didn't we? I mean, I stood up jist like you told me to."

"Yep, we teamed up. Listen, Reynolds, as soon as we reach Tucson, I'll be pullin' out for Magdalena myself. I'm going south to buy cattle. Now I can stop by this Adobe Wells and tell them you'll be a little late."

"Mr. Brannon, I hate to ask you this, but could you—I know you got better things to do—but could you deliver my letter to Rube? That way I won't be late with it."

Brannon pushed his hat to the back of his head. "Well, Read, if that letter of yours can slip into a saddlebag, and if I can find Adobe Wells, and if your friend just happens to be there when I ride by . . . I'd consider taking it."

"Be much obliged, Mr. Brannon. It's right there in my bag with the books and papers and—"

"Now hold on, Reynolds. I said I'd consider it. I've got to make arrangements in Tucson before I ride south. Then I'll come look you up and see if you still want me to take the letter."

"Be much obliged," Reynolds nodded. "Say, were you serious about me bein' the one to talk to the newspapers?"

"Yep."

Not much else was said until the train started to slow at the Tucson station.

"Mr. Gravette, I'd like to crack that door and hop down before we get to the crowd."

"I'm sorry, Mr. Brannon, but company policy prohibits—"

Brannon drew his revolver, spun the chambers, and then replaced it in his holster. "I thought you wanted to make sure there was no more gun play on your railroad. Now if these two dead outlaws have relatives waiting for them at the station, they just might try to take revenge right there on the platform."

"Oh," Gravette stewed, "I never . . . well, of course, just this one instance. I suppose jumping off a little early won't hurt anyone."

Brannon slid open the door, grabbed his satchel, and lunged for the platform. He hit the boards running, spurs jangling, and soon slowed up while the train slid on down to a waiting crowd.

As he expected, most saloons on the south side of town had emptied. People swarmed to the station to view what remained of the never-before-heard-of Matee Gang. Brannon filtered into the back side of the crowd, unrecognized.

Sauntering up to a familiar figure with black frock coat and stovepipe hat, Brannon drawled, "I say there, Lord Fletcher, it looks like a bloody mess!"

Jumping straight up and turning, Edwin Fletcher scowled, then laughed. "Stuart! I see you had to fight your way back into Arizona. My word, can't you even take a train ride without a shoot-out?"

Brannon shrugged, "That's my last train ride."

"Oh?"

"The S.P. thinks I'm bad for business."

"They may be right," Fletcher said with a laugh. "A rumor floated through town that you held off a dozen of them single-handedly."

"There were three of them, and one passenger got shot. Are you and Earl ready to pull out?"

"Right on schedule."

"Hardly," Brannon reminded the Englishman. "I was going to buy these cows last spring, remember?"

"Well, rebuilding the ranch buildings, an Apache uprising, and an unscheduled trip to Washington, D.C., tend to clutter a man's life."

The two men walked back toward a row of two-story buildings. "Did you and Earl bring everything from the ranch?"

"I know he brought the letters from Señora Pacifica, El Viento, and a pack horse to carry supplies."

"Who did Judge Quilici send to tend the ranch?"

"Fernandez, I believe."

"Ignacio's a good hand. Things ought to stay quiet for a while. Where's Earl?"

"At the livery, diamond-hitching that pack horse, I presume. Are we actually riding south today?"

"Just as soon as I get rid of these city clothes, check in with the sheriff, and pick up a letter from Reynolds."

"Who?"

"The old boy on the train who took a slug aimed for me. Told him I'd consider taking a letter to Mexico for him. It's right on the way."

"Are you going through another 'it-should-have-been-me' bout, as you did with Miss Cancino?" Fletcher pressed.

"Nope. Me and the Lord's come to terms with that, I suppose."

"Brannon, have you noticed how you make everything in life appear more and more theological?"

"Yep."

"That's it?"

"Yep."

"My word, I can just imagine the exciting conversation you had with the President. After a long, flowery speech about your virtues, he turned to you and said, 'Well, Mr. Brannon, would you be willing to head up the U.S. Marshal's office for Arizona Territory?' To which you replied, 'Nope.' Is that how it went?"

"Yep."

"Oh, I almost forgot," Fletcher added. "Did you have any luck at the Bureau of Indian Affairs? Could they locate Elizabeth?"

"You can imagine the runaround. I walked in there trying to locate a Nez Perce named Elizabeth with a small, half-breed son who was carried off to Indian Territory with Chief Joseph. The first thing they asked was her last name."

"She didn't have a last name," Fletcher said with a moan.

"Yeah, well tell that to a bureaucrat. Anyway, I did find out that some are still in I.T., some were sent to Washington Territory at the Coleville Reservation, and others were shipped to Florida."

"Florida? Why, in heaven's name, Florida?"

"To die of malaria, I suppose."

"You jest."

Brannon walked on. "Anyway, I sent a letter to all three locations, asking them to inform local agents of my desire to find Elizabeth."

"You've really done all you could."

"Yeah, well, it still doesn't settle well with me. I'm going to find her, Edwin. I won't stop until I do."

"Brannon, I'll tell you what your problem is. You figure Elizabeth is counting on you, and you somehow are letting her down. My word, there are times even the Brannon is unable to help."

"I'll figure out something," Brannon mumbled as he swung open the barn door and entered the stables.

Within an hour of the train's arrival, Brannon, Fletcher, and Earl Howland had their horses packed, clothes changed, and were ready to leave Tucson, but the stop at the sheriff's office took almost two hours. Fletcher and Howland were stretched out on the bench in front of the office when Brannon finally exited.

"We thought perhaps you'd been arrested," Fletcher teased as they cinched up their horses and mounted.

"For a while it was a real possibility. That railroad man, Gravette, told them the shooting was all my fault."

"Since when is self-defense a crime?" Fletcher quizzed.

"Well, it finally boils down to the fact that the sheriff would prefer I stay out of Tucson."

"Did he boot ya out of town, Mr. Brannon?"

"No, Earl. But he did let me know that he'd be mighty happy never to see me again."

"Well, I'll be . . . that just ain't—"

"Don't worry about it. Sheriffs come and go. Besides, I won't be coming this far south very often. Just let me get a herd back to the ranch, and I can sit there for a long time."

"Did you get that letter?" Fletcher asked.

"Yep. But I still don't know where Adobe Wells is. The sheriff had never heard of it, and it wasn't on any of his maps. I figure Señor y Señora Pacifica probably will know the place. Anyway, the sheriff didn't know anything about this Read Reynolds nor about Rube Woolsey."

"How far will we ride tonight?" Fletcher queried.

Brannon stood in the saddle and pointed south. "To La Paloma Blanca."

"The what?" Fletcher asked.

"The White Dove of the Desert—Mission San Xavier."

"How come they call that the White Dove?"

"You'll understand when you see it, Earl. You'll understand."

There were times when Stuart Brannon was sure Arizona was close to Heaven. *El Cielo Bueno!* April and May had more days like that than any other months. Groves of saguaro lifting limbs in praise. Sprinkled patches of cholla drooping in humble servitude. Bunched grass, green and thick. Greasewood laughing at the hot, dry winds. Cloudless skies, rugged horizons, crystal-clear vistas.

Flash floods, Indian raids, and drought could turn it into *El Infierno* . . . but not on this day. Brannon felt comfortable for the first time in two months. El Viento, his big, black horse, pranced beneath his saddle. His spurs jingled on his boots. His old hat was screwed down tightly, and his bandanna hung loosely around his neck.

Lord, it's a beautiful land. Stark, tough, made to last through the worst of conditions . . . and excellent in its simplicity. Kind of the way I'd like to be . . . but I'm not. I know it doesn't seem like I'm much good except for shootin' people. Surely You've got more for me to do in life than that.

The evening sun cast long shadows eastward, and the warm breeze died completely. The three men and four horses were climbing up the banks of a dry arroyo when Earl Howland in the lead gave a shout.

"Would you look at that?" he cried. "Ain't that a sight? One giant buildin' standin' out in the desert all by itself!"

"La Paloma Blanca, I presume," Fletcher exclaimed. "My word, Brannon, I've seen cathedrals in Europe smaller than that!"

"Mission San Xavier Del Bac . . . doesn't it shine?"

"It's monstrous! No trees, no village, no market—a person could see that white-washed building for fifty miles in any direction!"

"For almost a hundred years men have been riding across this valley and been startled by that church. Just when a man thinks he's miles beyond any law, La Paloma Blanca reminds him that he's accountable to a Higher Authority."

Brannon rode El Viento far to the east of the mission, tipped his hat to several shawl-covered ladies hurrying barefooted to answer the church bell's evening call, and stopped on a small bluff directly south of the building. The last streaks of sunlight reflected off the whitewashed bell towers, one of which remained unfinished. The air began to chill as the travelers made camp for the night.

All three men quietly sat around a small fire. The smoke spiraled straight up into the star-filled night.

"What made them do it, Mr. Brannon?"

"Do what, Earl?"

"You know, hike out into this desert a hundred years ago and build a church like that?"

"*Two* hundred years ago. That building is almost a hundred years old, but there was a church built before that."

Fletcher stretched around for another look. "My word, you don't say."

"Father Kino came into this area in 1692. Within a few years a church was built. Not many New England churches that can trace themselves back much further than that. So why did they do it? Missionary zeal, I suppose."

Fletcher swirled his boiled coffee in a tin cup. "Or the lust for power and profit."

"Well, there might've been a rattlesnake among them," Brannon responded, "but I've never met one."

"*¡Hola, Campamento! ¿Podemos entrar?*"

"*Adelante, amigos. Solamente hagan cierto que guardan sus manos lejos de sus cañones,*" Brannon called back.

"I say, Stuart, is this wise?"

Three men leading horses entered the glow of the campfire. They were caked with trail dust, and one limped so severely he needed to prop himself on his friend's shoulder.

Brannon waved toward the fire. "*No tenemos mas tazas y platos, pero si tienen utensilios, pueden servirse cafe y frijoles.*"

"What'd you tell them, Mr. Brannon?"

"To help themselves to some grub."

"*¡Gracias, Señor, muchas gracias!*"

"*¿Dónde van ustedes?*"

"A Colorado."

"*¿Porque?*"

"*Esperamos hallar mucho oro allí.*"

Brannon glanced at Howland and Fletcher. "They're heading to Colorado to try their hand at prospecting." He turned back to the visitors.

"*¿Como qué distancia han viajado?*"

"*Hemos viajado por once días. Pero hace dos días nuestras provisiones fueron robadas. Es verdad, fuimos afortunados de escapar con vida.*"

"Apaches?" Brannon quizzed.

"*No, eran—¿cómo se dice bandidos gringos?*"

"They got bushwhacked by a bunch of American outlaws who stole all their supplies."

The men scraped up the remaining food without speaking either to Brannon or to each other.

"What are they going to do without any supplies?" Fletcher asked.

"Maybe they've got relatives up in Tucson," Howland offered.

"*Compadres,*" Brannon began, "*¿cómo van a explorar en busca de minerales sin, ah . . . las herramientas correctas?*"

"*Tendremos que hallar trabajo primero, en Tucson.*"

"*¿Qué género de trabajo hacen ustedes?*"

"*Somos vaqueros.*"

"*¿Son buenos vaqueros?*"

"*Sí, Señor.*"

"Earl, do you feel as if we're being left out of this conversation?" Fletcher mused.

Brannon glanced impatiently at his two friends, then back at the vaqueros. "They're cowboys looking for some work until they replenish their food and gear."

"You thinking about putting them on?" Fletcher asked.

"Perhaps." Brannon looked at each one with a studied gaze. "¿*Habla Inglés?*"

The main spokesman smiled wide. "Yes," he said, "a little."

"Why on earth didn't you say so?" Brannon exclaimed with a laugh.

"You did not ask, Señor!"

"Where have you worked as cowboys?"

"We work all our lives on the big *ranchos* around Magdalena."

"Do you know Señor y Señora Pacifica?"

"Oh, yes, he was a very fine man, although we did not work for him. He will surely be missed."

"What do you mean, 'missed'?"

"Do you not know? Señor Pacifica was murdered early last summer."

"Oh, no!" Brannon moaned.

Fletcher rose to his feet, stammering, "M-my word!"

Earl Howland stood quickly and stepped over to Brannon. "Does this mean there won't be any cattle for us to buy?"

"How is Señora Pacifica? Does she still run the ranch?"

"Yes, she is a very strong lady."

"*¡Y muy hermosa!*" one of the other men added with a grin.

"We are going down to Magdalena to purchase many head of cattle from the Pacifica ranch and drive them north to my ranch. I'd like to hire you three for thirty dollars each. You'll get food and spare horses to ride. When we're through you'll be in northern Arizona with money in your pockets. Are you interested?"

The three men talked softly and rapidly to each other.

"Did you hire them?" Howland asked.

"They're thinking about it."

"Good heavens, Stuart, do you think you can trust them?"

"Well, we'll find out. Right now they're wondering whether they can trust us."

The spokesman turned to Brannon. "*Sí*, Señor, we would like to help Señora Pacifica and you." He held out his rough, calloused hand, and he and Brannon shook.

"What are your names?"

"Miguel."

"Jaime."

"Mateo."

"Well, this hombre is Earl Howland, the Englishman is Edwin Fletcher, and I'm Stuart Brannon."

"Brannon? This man is Brannon! We will be working for El Brannon?"

"*¿Proveerá balas extras?*" another asked.

"Yeah," Brannon muttered and nodded, "I'll furnish the extra bullets."

TWO

On the third evening south of Tucson, Miguel and Jaime brought back to camp six canteens filled with fresh water. They also brought two Apache boys.

"Stuart, we've got some company," Fletcher announced.

With one bare foot, Brannon stood and stepped gingerly toward the boys, carrying his boot. The taller, clad in a dirty cotton shirt and trousers, looked about ten. The other, wearing only a man's shirt that hung to his knees, was several years younger.

"Miguel, who are these boys?"

"They were at the river. They said they were lost and hungry."

Brannon glanced over at Fletcher and Howland.

"I ain't never heard of an Apache being lost," Earl chimed in. "Have you, Mr. Brannon?"

"Nope. But I've heard of many of 'em being hungry. Give them something to eat, Earl. Edwin, get Miguel and the others to pull their rifles and set guard at the perimeters."

"*¿El Brannon? ¡Este señor es El Brannon!*" one of the boys exclaimed.

Fletcher brushed his mustache with the back of his hand. "My word, Stuart, is there no end to your reputation?"

"*¿Habla Inglés?*"

"Yes," the little boy replied.

"What is your name?"

"Filippe."

"And what's your brother's name?"

"He is Cerdo."

"Pig?" Brannon puzzled.

"Yes, and it is a name that fits him well. Are you really El Brannon?"

"Filippe, I'll make a deal. I'll tell you the truth about who I am . . . and you tell me the truth about where your people are."

"Are you El Brannon?"

"Yes. Are you lost?"

"No. But we are alone, and we are hungry."

"Then eat . . . and we'll talk later."

Brannon pulled on his boot and walked out to Miguel who stood with his Winchester leaning casually over his shoulder and a quirley drooping from his lip.

"Did you find tracks of others at the creek?"

"These two came walking across the valley. If there are others, they are in those distant hills."

"Or in a hidden *barranca* only a few yards away?"

"That is always possible."

"If they aren't scouts, why are they here?"

Miguel let his hat slide back off his head and hang between his shoulders by the stampede string. "They would not tell me . . . but they might tell El Brannon."

"We'll bring the horses inside the circle tonight."

"And the boys?"

"I don't expect we could keep them here unless we hogtied them. If they want to go, they can go."

Earl Howland sauntered over to Brannon. "You going to let those boys stay in camp? They could steal us blind."

"Well, that would sure give the night guard something to do, wouldn't it?"

As Brannon walked back to the fire, he noticed that one of the boys had curled up on the dirt in the twilight shade by a small sage.

"Cerdo went to sleep?"

"He is very tired. His legs are not so long as mine."

The first stars were beginning to blink into view. Brannon sat down cross-legged and leaned against his saddle.

"Filippe, you told me you were not lost—so where are you going?"

"We are walking to the Sierra Madres."

"To Mexico?"

"Yes."

"Why?"

"We believe our grandfather, Cholla, is there."

"Cholla? The chief?"

"Yes."

"Where did you come from?"

"White Mountain."

Brannon stared at the bronzed, dirty face and deep, dark eyes. "You two have walked all this way?"

"Yes. Our father was killed in a fight with the soldiers, so they made us go to White Mountain. But we are Chiricahua. Those are not our people. So we left."

"You just walked off the reservation?"

"There was a battle at a spring with some gringos, and we hid in the brush. When the fight moved to the hills, we stayed behind."

"When was that?"

"Six days ago . . . I think."

"Have you had anything to eat for six days?"

"Yes, we are very good hunters. We shot some rabbits and snakes."

"Shot? With what?"

"Our bows and arrows."

"What bows?"

"We hid them at the creek because we did not want you to think that we came looking for a fight."

"Well, a couple of warriors like yourselves can't be too careful," Brannon said with a nod.

"Yes, you are right."

Filippe stood and walked over to where his brother lay sleeping. Suddenly he kicked his brother in the side. "Cerdo! Get up! We must leave camp!"

"Where are you going?" Brannon asked.

"We will not spend the night at your fire."

"Why not?"

"You might steal our things while we sleep."

"Steal your things?" Howland roared.

"Yes, 'The heart is deceitful, who can understand it?'"

"Good heavens, Brannon, the lad is quoting the Bible," Fletcher blurted.

"They might be a little primitive, but they aren't dumb," Brannon chided.

The boys started to walk out of camp.

"Filippe? How do I know that you are not returning to your people to tell them how to attack us?"

"We are only going to sleep over by the tall cactus. We want to stay and see the angels."

"Angels?" Fletcher quizzed.

"Yes. In the camps of the White River Apache, it is said that angels watch over Stuart Brannon. That is why he did not die at Apache Wells, or on the Prescott Road, or at San Pedro River. We want to see the angels."

"The angels probably are busy somewhere else tonight. If you two warriors are here in the morning, you're welcome to eat at our fire."

"Are you going to Mexico?" Filippe asked.

Brannon hesitated. "It would not be wise to tell of our plans."

Filippe and Cerdo quietly disappeared into the shadows as Earl Howland stirred the campfire.

"Do you believe them boys, Mr. Brannon?"

"They've never lied to me before."

"I don't trust 'em."

"Yeah, well, we'll keep two guards posted, and every man'll sleep with his boots on and his rifle in his hand."

"What else is new?" Fletcher teased. "Brannon doesn't rest well unless he's got someone out there taking potshots at him."

"Yeah," Howland sighed, "it does keep a fella from getting bored."

Coffee in a tin cup is either too hot or too cold. The secret, in Brannon's mind, was to let the heat warm your hands and the steam soothe your face until the exact moment the brew was barely cool enough to be drunk. Then it took about three quick gulps to empty the cup.

He sat cross-legged by the fire, debating whether the perfect moment for gulping the coffee had come, when Edwin Fletcher spoke.

"Say, Earl, how are those wedding plans coming?"

"I don't know nothin' about it. All Julie ever tells me is that I have to show up in a clean shirt and tie and say, 'I do.'"

"You really haven't set the date?"

"No, sir, Mr. Fletcher. All I know is that it will be two weeks to the day after we drive the cattle home. Julie said her and Miss Reed had it all planned out."

"So it seems . . . " Fletcher nodded. "Harriet refuses to discuss anything but the wedding. I've heard you have someone lined up to give the bride away."

Howland's smile stretched across his face and sparkled in the flicker of the firelight. "Yes, sir. Mr. Brannon agreed to walk her down the aisle."

"Earl, that is music to my ears," Brannon interrupted. "It hardly seems possible that Julie's able to walk. I thought that bullet might have crippled her for life."

"She's a very determined woman," Howland boasted.

"Spoken like a man about to be married," Fletcher added.

"Well, she still needs that cane," Howland continued. "But

she's determined to make it down the aisle with it. You know what else she told me, Mr. Brannon? She said that you get the first dance after the wedding. How do you like that?"

"I say, Brannon, when was the last time you went to Prescott? Harriet keeps asking about you. I'm afraid you've been terribly slack in your visitation."

"I hear there's an Englishman loitering about at the Bartons with his tongue hanging out."

"Yes, quite so. Trying to console another of the Brannon's castaways, I suppose. Actually, Stuart, you could stop by once in a while. I'm not sure she understands your behavior."

"You know, Edwin, I've got a feelin' that Harriet Reed understands me about as well as any woman ever did."

"Save one?" Fletcher raised his eyebrows.

Thoughts of Lisa danced lightly across Brannon's mind, and he gulped down cold coffee.

"Mr. Brannon, I ain't one to stir up old hurts," Earl began, "so if I'm out of place you jist sit me right down. But how did you know that Lisa was the right one to marry? I mean . . . you know, if you can remember back that far."

"Earl, I'm gettin' older by the minute. I'd say about now you're startin' to get a little worried. You're sayin' to yourself, 'Am I really able to make Julie the kind of husband she needs? Do I want to spend the rest of my life with this lady?'"

"Yeah . . . somethin' like that."

"Well, Earl, I have no idea in the world how a man knows for sure who to marry. The way I figure it is, you got to find a woman who wants to spend her life with you. Then you ask the Lord to help you be the kind of man she needs. After that, you make up your mind that you're going to stick it out no matter how much work it takes."

"I sure been thinkin' about it a lot lately."

"Well, don't over-think it."

"Over-think?"

"Like gold flakes in a pan . . . if you keep washin' them around long enough, they'll slop out with the sand."

Fletcher swung the coffeepot back and poured himself another cup. "I do say, Howland, the days for deciding are past. Neither Julie Cancino—nor Miss Harriet Reed for that matter—would let you back out now."

Brannon grabbed a biscuit from the pan and tossed it at Howland. "Edwin's right. No reason for a hooked fish to debate whether to bite the bait."

Earl Howland stood and packed his rifle over his right shoulder. "I'll go relieve Mateo." He walked to the outer edge of the firelight, then whirled and blurted, "Mr. Brannon? Do you think you'll ever get married again? Julie and me was talkin', and she said she doubted it, but I ain't too sure. A man gets mighty lonely livin' by himself . . . mighty lonely."

Brannon sprang to his feet so quickly that it startled both Fletcher and Howland.

"My word, what is it?" Fletcher exclaimed. "Do you hear something?"

"Them Apaches. It's them Apaches, ain't it?" Howland added.

"No . . . no . . . just sort of, you know, a cramp in my leg. I'd better stretch it out. I'll go relieve Mateo, Earl. You and Fletcher can stay by the fire and discuss nuptial bliss."

"I do say, Earl, I believe he's running from your inquiry."

Stuart Brannon didn't hear the comment. He didn't hear what Mateo said when he relieved him on guard. He didn't even know what he had replied. His mind had drifted back to Lisa. And to another trip to Mexico.

After a few moments, Edwin Fletcher stepped to his side. "Stuart, you've got young Howland worried sick. He didn't mean any hardship for you."

"I know. I'm too sensitive. Harriet made that quite clear. She's right, you know."

"So," Fletcher cleared his throat, "what memories haunted you this time?"

"Did I ever tell you about Bomista's bull? I can't believe the two of us rode two hundred miles into Mexico for a bull! It was all Lisa's idea. She met me at the barn rattling on about Teresa's grandfather's brother's bull!

"The calves were reported to be the largest, strongest, healthiest, sturdiest ones in all of Sonora. So we saddled up Sage and Roanie and rode south in the middle of June! Lord, we were just too happy to be scared and too dumb to worry.

"It was the dirtiest Lisa ever got in her life! Her face smeared, her dress caked with mud. Her hair—that had to be the worst rat's nest I've ever seen. I'm glad I never told her that.

"There was supposed to be a beautiful hacienda. We found an adobe cabin. He owned thousands of head of cattle, we were told. But we saw only fifty. They said he had servants to wait on him hand and foot. We saw only Jose.

"Bomista. Antonio Rafael Bomista. Cattle buyer, horse trader, land developer . . . crook. Tobacco juice on his beard and dribbling down his vest. With a less than gentle mix of aromas of cheap whiskey, dried sweat, and cow manure.

"Lisa had planned on hugging him once for Teresa, but settled for a distant hand shake.

"'Go and get El Toro Bomista!' he shouted in Spanish to Jose.

"'And which bull is that?' Jose asked.

"'The first one you catch!' Bomista hollered.

"I don't believe that he ever knew I spoke Spanish. And Lisa was so thrilled to have found the perfect bull. What could I do? El Toro Bomista—1,800 pounds of the most worthless bovine ever produced on the North American continent.

"'Two hundred dollars,' Bomista insisted. 'He is like one of the family!'

"'He's not worth fifty, and you know it!' I said.

"'Stuart!' Lisa gasped.

"'Sold for fifty,' Bomista grinned. 'Any friend of Teresa's is just like family to me!'

"'He will follow you home like a puppy,' Bomista promised.

"On the second day, the 'puppy' broke the rope, tried to gore Sage, and ran off into the sand dunes. It took us all afternoon to pull him out of there and get back on the trail.

"'Serves you right,' Lisa scolded. 'You probably insulted El Toro Bomista when you paid such a lamentable price for him.'

"'Insulted him? Lisa, you have the . . .'"

Brannon's musings halted. He thought he heard a noise in the shadows of night. He squatted on his haunches and quietly cocked his rifle.

There it is. A whistle? A signal? A . . . snore?

Quietly he walked ahead about twenty paces and then stood perfectly still trying to make out the figures on the ground ahead of him. Fletcher, revolver drawn, stepped up beside him.

"Filippe? Cerdo? Sleep, *niños,* sleep well."

Returning to the fire this time, Brannon easily lapsed back into the story of Lisa and the bull.

"The next day we tried driving the bull ahead of us, but when he wasn't charging the horses, he was trying to run off into the brush. Finally we dallied him to both saddles. We almost had to drag him to Tucson. I figured a week on the trail would settle him down, so we pulled off the ropes when we neared Phoenix—and he immediately ran off and hid in the banks of the Salt River.

"That's where the snake spooked Roanie, Lisa bucked off, I shot the snake, and El Toro Bomista disappeared over the horizon. It took us two days to track him down, about halfway to Florence. I tossed a rope on him there, and before I had time to dally, he jerked me right out of the saddle.

"Well, now, being drug through the cactus isn't my favorite activity, but Lisa's screamin', 'Don't let go, Stuart! Don't let go!'

"Right at that moment I remember thinkin' how much I wish I had my Winchester in my hand. El Toro Bomista would have become El Toro Muerto.

"I let go, of course, and that bull disappeared over the rim with my best rawhide. I believe I bruised every bone in my body . . . and Lisa is sitting up there on Roanie yelling, 'Why did you let him go?' I don't know why, but I rolled over on my back and just stared up at her.

"When she slowed down a bit, I started to say something, but began laughing. I mean, I busted loose and couldn't stop. Soon as I'd cup a mouthful of air, away I'd go again. Well, pretty soon, Lisa was busting up, too.

"'Stuart,' she cackled, 'you must be the dirtiest man in the West. Now I know why Bomista looked like that—he spent his life trying to catch that bull!'"

Brannon sighed and started to laugh. Then Fletcher followed. Soon Howland and the others joined in.

"Stuart," Fletcher choked as he sucked air, "Stuart, I don't think I've ever seen you laugh this hard!"

"That's what it would take," Brannon gasped.

"I say . . . what?"

"A woman who could make me laugh this hard!"

Most of the men grabbed another cup of coffee.

"You still want a perimeter guard?" Howland finally asked.

"Nope."

"Why not?"

"Those boys are sleeping about twenty feet west of us. They aren't going to warn anyone tonight. We'll just keep one guard—like before. Earl, you take the first shift, and I'll have Mateo take the second. I don't know about you boys, but I'm turnin' in."

He still was chuckling as he unfastened his bedroll.

"I say, Brannon, you didn't finish the story."

"About the bull?"

"Quite. Surely the fabled Stuart Brannon didn't walk away from an inhospitable bovine."

"Yes and no. I told Lisa that Bomista said the bull would follow us like a puppy, and that's the one thing we hadn't tried. So I told her we were going home, and the bull could just follow us.

"Well, we sank the spurs into our horses and took her at a lope for most of the afternoon. We stopped for the night at the top of

Pine Ridge, and I'll be if Lisa didn't look back down the trail and spot old Bomista Bull!

"That's the way it went for the next two days. Then, just before we hit Sunrise Creek Valley, he disappeared."

"Around the Quilici Ranch?"

"The lower end of it. Anyway, I figured we'd finally lost him. So we get to the ranch and clean up. All evenin', Lisa walks out to the porch to look for that bull, but he doesn't show up. Lisa wanted me to go back and look for him, but I refused. She fussed for a few days, but then we got busy with other things.

"Lisa spent three days puttin' in the garden, and I'm up on the ridge doctorin' some sick cows. You know, up by the spring.

"Well, I'm ridin' home and hear a rifle shot from the direction of the house, so I gallop into the yard. As far as I know, that's the only time she ever fired a gun in her life.

"Anyway, I ride into the yard and there, sprawled out in her fresh garden, deader than a nail, is old El Toro Bomista—with my rawhide still draggin' around his neck.

"By the time I get to the house, Lisa's in the kitchen cookin' supper like nothin' had happened.

"'Stuart,' she says, 'an 1,800-pound pile of manure just ripped up every inch of my garden. Would you go out there and bury it right where it lays? At least we can get fifty dollars worth of fertilizer out of it.'

"So I did. Later that night we were sittin' out on the porch and not talkin' much. 'Someday, Stuart, our grandchildren will ask why we call that piece of ground Bomista Memorial Gardens.' We must have laughed until midnight.

"Yep, Edwin, someday I'll tell my grandchildren . . . "His voice trailed off.

"Someday, Stuart, you'll find a woman who'll make you laugh again," Fletcher said quietly.

Earl Howland was scraping bacon and beans around in a smoking black frying pan over a fire when Brannon returned to camp aboard El Viento.

"Any sign of them?"

"Nope. They even brushed out the tracks of where they slept. I trust they headed back to White Mountain."

"You don't believe that, do you?" Fletcher countered as he approached the fire.

"Nope."

Fletcher pointed. "My guess is that's them right up on the knoll."

Brannon stood in the stirrups and saw Filippe and Cerdo ambling toward them. Cerdo appeared to be carrying a rabbit.

"Where did they come from? I didn't see them out there."

"Looks like they've got breakfast," Howland observed.

Brannon swung down out of the saddle. "You boys went huntin' early," he called.

"We have eaten ours already," Filippe answered, pointing to the rabbit. "This is for you. Cerdo ate many beans and biscuits last night and wants to pay you back."

"Certainly you boys can keep—"

Brannon interrupted Fletcher. "Thank you. You boys must be fine hunters. Did you shoot it with your arrows?"

"Yes, Cerdo shot this one."

Earl Howland, carrying a plate of fried meat, looked over at the boys. "Come on, Brannon, those little bows are just toys . . . aren't they?"

"I have a feeling that they are very good shots," Brannon surmised.

"I say, you'd have to sneak right up on top of a rabbit to hit him with such a lightweight outfit," Fletcher commented.

"It just might be that you're underestimating these boys," Brannon cautioned. "Cerdo? How would you like a biscuit?"

The boy nodded.

"I'm going to toss this biscuit in the air. If you hit it with your arrow, you can have it."

Without another word, Brannon tossed the biscuit about ten feet above his head. Instantly two arrows whizzed through the sourdough, both holding fast at the feathers.

The boys left the rabbit, took the biscuit and another that Brannon offered and then sauntered out into the sage.

"Are you going back to White Mountain?"

"We are going to our grandfather."

"My word," Fletcher gasped, "we certainly can't let them go out there on their own!"

"We don't have any other choice," said Brannon. Then he called out, "Filippe and Cerdo, you are welcome to eat at our campfire."

Cerdo turned toward Brannon, nodded, and then walked on. Suddenly Filippe glanced back and shouted, "The Brannon is always welcome at our campfire as well!"

The trail across the desert wound down through arroyos and up over mesas as the men and their horses plodded along. Finally they broke out into a flat desert valley. The sun was almost straight up, and they had seen no sign of the boys since daylight. Then Brannon noticed a cloud of dust on the far-off mountain horizon. As he pointed, two quick shots rang out from a distant rifle.

THREE

Are we goin' to go take a peek at that?" Howland ventured. Brannon pulled his Winchester from its scabbard. "Not until we know a little more."

Fletcher turned in the saddle on his mahogany bay gelding. "How many do you suppose there are?"

"I heard only one rifle."

"But two shots," countered Howland, standing in the stirrups as he gazed across the desert floor to the outlying hills.

Jaime, hat dangling by the stampede string and bouncing on his back, rode up to Brannon.

"El Viejo, I believe that is the direction of the two Apache boys."

"What did he call you?" Fletcher asked. "Doesn't *viejo* mean old?"

"The boys call me the Old Man, just like they do the foreman of any ranch in Texas. Miguel thinks that's the direction the Indian boys headed."

"But they don't have a rifle," Fletcher stated.

"Nope. That's why we'll take a little excursion. Someone might be taking shots at them."

"Maybe they're already dead," Howland offered.

Another shot echoed across the desert . . . then another.

"Well, someone's still shootin', so not everyone's dead," said

Brannon. Then in two languages he commanded, "Pull your rifles—and let's take it slow and easy."

If he had known for sure it was the boys, if he had known the strength of the attacker, if he had known their position, Brannon might have spurred El Viento and raced to the rescue. Instead, he led the men in a slow, methodical path, keeping a low profile on the desert floor.

An occasional shot rang out from the rock of the treeless hills, but Brannon could distinguish only a single gun. As they reached the base of the mountains, the ground sloped down to a huge field of rock and boulders. Brannon held back the others and surveyed the scene.

At first the bright noontime sun reflected by the granite blinded him. Brannon wondered if an ancient lava flow had lapped right up to the granite, then receded. But his reverie was broken by a puff of smoke, an explosion, and what sounded like a curse.

Brannon rubbed the thick stubble of his unshaven face and brushed away a pesky fly.

"There he is," he murmured to the others. "There's a buck-skin horse tied at the sage on the right, and he's propped up on a boulder at the back."

"Just one?" Howland asked.

"So it seems."

Fletcher took a swig from his canteen and looped it back over the saddle horn. "What is he hunting in those rocks?"

"Don't know, but I doubt he's spotted us yet."

"The Apache boys!" Miguel pointed as he whispered.

"The boys? Where?" Brannon strained to see.

"They are out of sight now."

"We're moving in. Miguel, you, Jaime, and Mateo slip around to that sage and grab his horse. Don't let him escape. Edwin, you, me, and Earl will ride right up on him like we're just coming down the trail. Don't get too anxious to shoot. There might be a good explanation for this."

What had looked like a mere field of stones at the edge of the lava turned out to be broken walls of what once had been a small, fortified village. Not one building remained, and the erosion of wind and weather had obliterated all traces of habitation. Only a few straight lines of forgotten adobe architecture divulged the past.

Brannon glanced at the ruins and then trained his eyes on the man with the rifle near the well. The bushy-bearded man removed his wide Spanish hat and waved them in. They circled the stone and broken adobe and approached the stranger cautiously. He wore shotgun chaps, ragged at the boot. He reached into his brown leather vest and pulled out a plug of tobacco. Only when he spoke did Brannon guess his nationality.

"Welcome, boys . . . and help yourself to a chaw of tobaccy! You jist driftin' down the trail, or you lookin' for someone in particular?"

"We're goin' down into Mexico to visit a friend," Brannon replied. He tilted his black hat back with his left hand, but kept his right hand on the Winchester.

"Well, you're in Mexico right here, friend!"

"We crossed the border?" Howland questioned.

"Yep." The man spat tobacco juice over on the rocks. "Used to be a little town here years ago. But since it ended up so close to the border, no one bothered to rebuild it."

"This wouldn't be called Adobe Wells, would it?" Brannon asked.

"Why, yes, sir, it is! The well still has some water in it, though it's mostly caved in. It's over behind that sage where I hitched my horse."

The man finally noticed Miguel and the other two parked at the sage.

"Hey! Them Mexicans is tryin' to steal my horse!" he yelled, lifting his rife.

Instantly Brannon's Winchester was pointed at the man's head.

"Drop it, Mister!" he shouted.

"You partnerin' with them Mexican horse thieves?" he accused, lowering his rifle.

"Drop it on the rocks!" Brannon growled.

"You're makin' a big mistake!"

Brannon's shot sailed harmlessly into the desert sand about a foot to the left of the man's feet. Immediately the man dropped his rifle.

"And the revolver," Brannon ordered.

"You're in a peck of trouble, stranger. They hang horse thieves around here."

"We're not stealing your horse—those boys ride for me. We were just ridin' by and heard the shots. You sure seem to be in a hurry to waste bullets."

"You ain't goin' to steal anything from me?"

"Nope. But we don't intend to get shot by a jumpy trigger finger neither. You signaled us in, remember?"

"I thought you was somebody else. I been waitin' for a friend to show."

"You target practicing, or what?"

He grinned wide and flashed a yellow-toothed smile. "Huntin' rabbits!"

"Rabbits in those rocks?"

"Yep. Got two of them flushed in there. Soon as they pop up I'll finish them off. Maybe you boys would like to hep out?"

"Are you sure those are rabbits in there?" Fletcher interrupted.

"He's an Englishman, ain't he?"

"So goes the rumor," Brannon nodded. "Mister, I'm lookin' for two little Apache boys. Have you seen them?"

"'Course I've seen 'em! I told you I was huntin' rabbits, didn't I?"

Brannon swung down from El Viento and let the reins drop. The barrel of his rifle was only inches from the man's head.

"You were shooting at those boys?" he grilled.

"I ain't shootin' at no boys. No, sir, I'm shootin' 'Paches."

The barrel of Brannon's rifle jabbed the man just above the sternum, causing him to stagger back among the boulders.

"Mister, you're shootin' at little boys . . . and they hang men for that in every country on earth," Brannon snarled. "Earl, hogtie this snake before I get really mad."

Turning his gaze across the rocks and ruins he called out, "Filippe! Cerdo! It's all right; come on out!"

First one head and then another popped up from the rocks. Filippe stood and helped his brother to his feet. They cautiously picked their way across the jagged rocks toward Brannon and the others.

"You didn't take any bullets, did you?"

"No. He is not a very good shot," Filippe called.

"How in the world did you let such a worthless fellow get the drop on you?"

"Cerdo was singing, and I did not hear the horse breathe."

"Singing?"

"Yes," Cerdo grinned, "about tortillas filled with brown sugar and dates!"

"Well, why didn't you shoot this gunman with your arrows?" Fletcher questioned.

"We thought perhaps he was a friend of El Brannon."

"No one who shoots at little boys is a friend of mine."

"Brannon?" the bound man coughed. "Stuart Brannon from up in Yavapai County?"

"You got a point to make, Mister? Then make it."

"Mr. Brannon, look, I didn't know it was you. I had no idea in the world them boys were friends of yours. I wouldn't have taken a gun to them under no circumstances whatever if I hadda knowed. There ain't a durn fool in the Territory—or in old Mexico—who'd try to cross ya, 'lessin he was drunk . . . and I ain't drunk. 'Course, I do drink some. We all do, now don't we? But I ain't drunk, no, sir. Though I once heard that Stuart Brannon never touched likker. Is that right, or was that jist a nasty rumor?"

"Mister, I'm going to stick that little barrel cactus in your mouth if you don't swallow those words and keep still for a minute."

Brannon turned to Filippe. "Now are you boys headin' out with us, or are you going on your own?"

"We do not need anyone's help," Filippe boasted.

"Then you two scoot on out of here, and we'll keep this coyote roped up for a while. Cerdo, quit singing so loud."

Brannon looked down at the sparkling eyes of an otherwise filthy boy. Cerdo nodded his head in agreement. Brannon dug in his saddle bag and pulled out two pieces of beef jerky and tossed them to the boys. "Now go find your grandfather, and stay away from hombres like this."

In half a minute the boys had disappeared from sight.

"I say, Brannon, isn't this the place you were to deliver the letter from that chap in Tucson?"

"Reynolds's letter . . . Adobe Wells!"

"Reynolds!" the roped man exclaimed. "You know Read Reynolds?"

"Somehow I get the feeling you're Rube Woolsey."

"Yes, sir, Mr. Brannon, I'm Rube. Where's Read?"

"In a hotel in Tucson with a bad gunshot wound."

"Did he lose the letter?"

"Nope, I brought it for him."

"You got the letter then?"

"Yep."

"Is Read goin' to live?"

"That's what the doctors say."

"That's good, that's mighty good. I've knowed Read since the beginning of the war. Ain't seen him in years though. We been fightin' in different locations."

"War?" said Fletcher. "There's a war on down here? I haven't read of any Mexican war."

"The war of freedom for the Confederacy!" Woolsey spouted.

"That war's been over for fifteen, eh, sixteen years," Howland blurted.

"It ain't over 'til we all give up, and we ain't give up. You understand, don't you, Brannon? I hear your sympathies were for the South."

"My sympathies were for Texas."

"Same thing."

"Not to Sam Houston, it wasn't."

"Captain Porter says Houston was a traitor."

"Mister, this is the second time today my trigger finger has wanted to put lead through you. I'm beginnin' to run out of excuses why not to."

"Look, I ain't doin' too good with all this palaver. So just cut me loose, give me my letter, and I'll whip on out of here."

"Mr. Brannon, you want us to noon it over by the well?" Howland asked.

"Yep."

"How about this snake?"

"He can siesta 'til we're ready to leave."

Woolsey rolled over and glared up at Brannon. "You cain't do this! You got to feed me dinner!"

"Edwin," Brannon mused, "did you hear a squeaking sound?"

Fletcher smiled. "Didn't hear a thing."

They ate tortillas wrapped around salted meat and green peppers. Then they repacked the supplies. Brannon picked up a small shovel and returned to check on the bound man.

"These rocks is hard, Brannon. Cut me loose!"

"Afraid not, Woolsey. I want to make sure those boys get a good head start."

"You ain't going to dig me no grave, is ya?" Woolsey cried.

"Nope."

Next to a sage, Brannon dug a hole in the ground about one

foot wide and three feet deep. He tied a large, flat rock to one end of a short rope, dropped the rock into the hole, and then slowly refilled the hole with dirt, tamping it thoroughly.

"You going to rock-hobble him?" Howland asked as he led El Viento over to Brannon.

"Yep."

"You cain't do that! I ain't done nothin'. There ain't no law in Mexico against shootin' Apaches!"

"I don't know about that, Woolsey, but there are higher laws than what any government makes." Brannon tied Woolsey's bound hands to the free end of the short rope.

"Even the Almighty don't come down here," Woolsey sneered. "This is the devil's territory."

"You're wrong, Woolsey. The Lord must be here, or I would have shot you dead long before now."

"I'll starve to death out here," he protested.

"Nope. You've got water, food, guns, ammunition, a bear knife sixteen inches long, and transportation over at that horse."

"But the rope's too short. I cain't get to my horse tied up like this!"

"You're right. I'd suggest you dig out that rock first, then pack it over to your saddle, pull that blade, and cut yourself free."

"Dig out that rock? You goin' to leave me that shovel?"

"Nope."

"I cain't dig out that rock with my bare hands. It would take me all afternoon!"

"No, it'll take you about two hours, depending on how tough your hands are. By that time we'll be down the road . . . and so will those boys."

"You cain't do that!" Woolsey cried as they turned to ride away.

"Mr. Fletcher, is there a law against rock-hobbling polecats in Mexico?" Brannon inquired.

Fletcher shook his head, grinned, and spurred the mahogany

bay. "I don't suppose I should ask how you know it takes only two hours to dig out that rock."

"Nope." Brannon trotted El Viento to the lead.

The next two days turned routine.

Hot.

Dusty.

Meager landscape.

No towns.

Very few travelers.

Miguel knew all the springs and creeks.

Howland cooked and complained about the flies.

Fletcher discussed the superiority of the American political system, the escape of Billy the Kid from the Lincoln County Jail, the morality of the Chinese Exclusion Treaty, and Miss Harriet Reed.

Brannon argued the benefits of dehorning range steers.

But no one listened.

And every night at sunset, Filippe and Cerdo wandered into camp in time to eat beans and biscuits.

"I say, Stuart, how is it that we ride horseback all day and never see any sign of those lads, yet they pop out of the desert every evening in time for supper?"

"Relays."

"What?"

"You see," Brannon teased, "every Apache boy in Mexico looks like Filippe and Cerdo. So they station them every twenty-five or thirty miles. We're dining with a new pair every evening and don't know it."

"That's a pathetic response," Fletcher chided.

Brannon nodded. "We got two very tough kids here."

"You wouldn't be thinking of hiring them for the Triple B, would you?"

"If they show up at the door in about ten years, they've got a job."

As they turned into the foothills, the desert receded and grassland increased. Brannon noticed that most of the northern slopes were still green. Filippe and Cerdo no longer came at mealtime.

We'll have to bring the cattle along by the mountains . . . then push out to Adobe Wells . . . up to the Santa Cruz . . . then on to Tucson . . . maybe we can find a box canyon full of grass and fatten them up before the desert . . . .

"El Viejo!" Miguel called. "El Rancho Pacifica!"

"*¿Dónde?*"

"On the *mesa verde,* see? It is a beautiful *rancho.*"

"Is that it?" Howland asked.

"Yep," Brannon nodded.

"Where's the cattle?"

"I was wondering the same thing myself. Maybe they have other ranges."

"Miguel, where do they keep the *vacas?*"

"*¿Quien sabe?* Perhaps they sold them."

"That's encouraging." Brannon shrugged at Howland.

Brannon took the lead once more and trotted El Viento up the long drive to the walled, tree-lined hacienda. The sun gleamed low in the west, and the breeze felt softly cool after many days in the desert.

A man can look fifty miles in every direction from here. The cattle will be mountain tough and meadow fat. Lord, you must enjoy slipping down here in the evenin's. Beautiful . . . refreshing . . . peaceful.

At the first crack of rifle fire Brannon dove to the dirt, dragging his Winchester with him. Three more shots and a shout convinced him it had been a warning. El Viento and all the men had retreated to safety, but Brannon continued to cower in the dirt.

"*Amigo, ¿porqué nos dispara a nosotros? ¿Habla Inglés?*"

"Go away!"

"May I please speak to Señora Pacifica?" Brannon shouted.

"She does not want to talk to you. You must leave or we will shoot you."

"I have traveled far in order to buy her cattle."

"You have traveled far in order to *steal* her cattle."

"I do not see any cattle. Are they on other ranges?"

"Many have been stolen by gringos such as yourself. If you will not leave, we must shoot you!"

"Please tell La Señora that Mr. Stuart Brannon of Yavapai County, Arizona, would like to speak with her."

"El Brannon? Which of you is El Brannon?"

"I am Stuart Brannon!"

"Yes, and I am Simón Bolívar. Last week in Magdalena there was a gunfight. Two gringos, both claiming to be El Brannon, shot each other in the street."

"I know nothing of Magdalena. I want to speak to Victoria Maria Alezon Fuentes-Delgado Pacifica. Tell her I sorrow for her on the death of Don Rinaldo—and ask her how is the health of her father, the Vice-General of Monterrey? Tell her I am the man who buried Enrique, and I hope I will not have to bury any more of her faithful workers!"

There was a long span of silence, though sounds of people scurrying behind the wall filtered down to Brannon.

"Stuart, what's going on?" Fletcher yelled.

"Something happened to scare them, Edwin. They're just being cautious."

Fletcher slowly rode his horse toward Brannon with El Viento in tow. "I trust it is not a revolution or a land grant claim."

Finally two heavy oak doors, each about eight feet wide, swung open, and a woman with flowing black hair, wearing a long black dress, swooped out of the yard.

"Señor Brannon! This lack of hospitality is inexcusable! Please, please arise—you are welcome always at this ranch. Our caution is well-founded but sad."

"Señora Pacifica," Brannon replied grinning, "this is Edwin Fletcher, my partner in the cattle business; Earl Howland, my foreman; and Miguel, Jaime, and Mateo who also work for me."

"You will be guests in the big house," she insisted.

"Mr. Brannon, me and the boys will find us a cot in the bunkhouse," Howland asserted. "We'll take care of the horses."

Señora Pacifica immediately began to issue orders.

"Felicia, please bring fruit and cheese to the table by the oak— these men will rest there. Roberto, prepare the pit for a roast. We will have pork. And tell Bustado to prepare a fine meal for everyone. Tonight will be fiesta. And please have Juan close the gates immediately."

"Mr. Brannon, despite such an unpleasant reception, we are delighted to have you at our *rancho*." She turned with a frown to the servants who had not left for their assignments.

"*¿Que pasa?*" she queried.

Finally, one of the men spoke. "Is this man really El Brannon?"

"Yes, I have told you many times of our friendship."

"I think . . . some did not always believe you."

"Mr. Brannon, it is embarrassing for me to ask, but would you mind shaking hands with my people so they can go back to work? They would like to meet El Brannon."

Brannon hemmed and hawed. "El Brannon, eh? I think maybe someone is tryin' to play a little prank here."

"Perhaps you are unaware that Hawthorne Miller's books have been translated into Spanish? Felicia reads them every Sunday evening."

"How many books are there?"

"Twelve, of course."

"Twelve!" Fletcher said, whistling. "My word, Brannon, you simply must read them and find out what you are going to do next."

Brannon greeted each of the workers and then turned back to Victoria.

"Señora . . . if I might be so bold . . . I was deeply saddened to hear of your husband's death. May I ask how it happened?" Brannon suddenly found himself drawn to her magnetic eyes.

"It occurred last summer. A dozen of Captain Porter's men showed up wanting to buy some cattle."

"The renegade Confederate? He wanted to buy cattle?"

"Yes, they said they had money."

"And your husband refused?"

"Don Rinaldo was a very principled man—much like you, I suspect, Mr. Brannon. He told them that he did not support their cause and demanded that they leave the ranch.

"They left. But the next morning, as we came out of the chapel, two shots were fired from the top of the wall near the carpenter's shop. One bullet hit Don Rinaldo in the chest, the other in the neck."

Her head bent down for a moment as Brannon searched for some comforting word. He found none.

She gave a deep sigh. "He died in my arms as I sat under that oak tree." She looked again at Brannon, tears streaming down her cheeks.

"Last year in the creek bed in southern Utah, I thought I would lose him to the ambushers. But you came along and saved us. But this year . . . this year there was no Brannon to protect . . . only angels to take him home. Please forgive my tears. It is most difficult to feel so helpless when a loved one dies in your arms."

Brannon quickly turned his face away from her and tried to relieve the tightness in his chest.

"Now if you will excuse me for a moment, do make yourself at home."

For a few minutes, neither of the men moved. Finally Fletcher stepped over and put his hand on Brannon's shoulder. "Stuart, this is a rather lovely ranch, wouldn't you say?"

Brannon glanced around at the spacious yard, the sprawling house, the corrals with waiting horses, the immense barn. "You know, Edwin, without the walls this place would be a replica of what Lisa and I wanted to build on the Sunrise Creek Ranch. Garden, orchard, milk cows, chickens, tannery, blacksmith's shop, chapel . . . look at that chapel! It's self-contained. It's ideal!"

"Except," Fletcher reminded him, "for the fact that you need armed guards at the wall and you hardly dare venture outside."

Brannon nodded. "Yeah. She hasn't explained all that."

"She is an extremely handsome woman."

Brannon lifted his eyebrows. "You noticed?"

"My word, yes, I noticed. But the amazing thing is that Stuart Brannon noticed. Don't tell me there is an ounce of warm blood stirring in that cold heart of yours."

Sometime after washing up, while Fletcher and Brannon relaxed in stretched rawhide chairs and slowly savored sweet oranges, Señora Pacifica rejoined the men.

"Please excuse my absence. There were arrangements to make. I have sent some men to notify Ramon."

"How is your brother? Is he still angry about what I did to him in Tres Casas?" *She moves so quickly, so fluidly, like a Spanish Lisa.*

"Perhaps, but face-to-face in a fight with El Brannon . . . and survive. Well, Ramon has made the story almost a legend."

"Is he far?"

She is the queen in this domain, but a benevolent one. She rules with a glance of the eye, a sparkle in the voice, a tilt of the head.

"He and most of the *vaqueros* were driving cattle to summer pasture. I'm afraid we lost to Captain Porter's thieves the herd we had saved for you. We will bring some of the others back for you."

She can dance . . . oh, I'm sure she can dance.

"Have you heard much about your Captain Porter?"

Brannon jerked straight up. "*My* Captain Porter?"

"An American. He and the others came here after the war. They claimed to be building an army for the reconquest of the South."

"Good heavens!" Fletcher flung his hands in the air. "I still can't believe they refuse to give up!"

"Well, that was their excuse for banditry for years. Their group has dwindled to only a few men, and now they claim to be revolutionaries intending to 'liberate' Baja California. But even that effort has failed to gain support. About a dozen men showed up to collect a donation for the liberation of Baja."

"They rustled your cattle?"

"Four days ago on Sunday. As I said, most of the men were in the high mountains. The others had taken their families into the village on Saturday night and stayed over for Sunday mass. Only a few had remained here when the bandits arrived."

"Why didn't your workers stay here for church?" Brannon asked. "Are they not allowed to attend your chapel?"

"Oh, yes, they may all attend. But, of course, most are Roman Catholic."

"And you?" Brannon asked.

"Protestant. I once told you that my story would surprise you."

"My word . . . a Protestant out in this country," Fletcher muttered.

"Methodist, actually," she nodded. "But all of that is a very long story. Anyway, we held them out of the hacienda, but could do nothing to keep them from stealing the cattle."

"I think, with your permission, I would like to attempt to bring back your herd," Brannon offered.

"Oh, no! It would be dangerous. I could never let you."

"Señora Pacifica," Fletcher interjected, "I very much doubt if you could stop him from trying. Stuart, here, sees it as his divine destiny to champion difficult causes."

"Your divine destiny, Mr. Brannon? Do you take your faith seriously?"

"Most assuredly," Fletcher answered for him. "Only please, don't ask him any theological questions. We once spent six days debating the depravity of man."

"How many men could you spare to ride with us?" Brannon queried.

"You are serious, aren't you?"

"I sure am, Señora."

"Please call me Victoria. With so many of my men in the mountains, I believe I could send out no more than four or five. But I must admit, they are not excellent gunmen like the fabled El Brannon."

"Call me Stuart. Only in storybooks is there an El Brannon."

FOUR

Brannon and Fletcher reposed in the shade of the sprawling oak, guzzling strong, thick coffee. They calmly surveyed the bustle of activity around them.

Several young boys strung lanterns throughout the courtyard. Women with deep creases around their eyes swept the baked dirt yard. Children scooped up chickens to return them to the hen house. Dogs scampered and barked. A huge black and white cat sat on the roof of the big house, ignoring the entire scene.

The air was peppered with shouts of command, good-natured retorts, and laughter. Much laughter.

"Brannon, these people—these Mexicans—they have a great ability to celebrate and enjoy life."

"I was thinking the same thing. They just lost 850 head of cattle. El Patron was shot last summer. They might be under attack at any moment. Yet tonight it's fiesta time!"

"The Celts are that way, you know. It must be our cold Anglo-Saxon blood," Fletcher mused.

Brannon nodded.

Lord, I sure could learn a lot from these folks. Everything is always a crisis with me. Lisa perpetually told me that. Even Elizabeth noticed it. Velvet maintained the same. As did Rose . . . and Harriet. Well, I'm not going to look for lost cattle tonight . . . so I'll celebrate . . . it's fiesta!

"I say, Brannon, I believe Señora Pacifica has invited in the neighbors." Fletcher motioned toward a fringed carriage that had just rolled into the yard. Exiting the coach were two women wearing brightly-colored silk dresses and several gentlemen in frock coats. Several armed guards escorted them.

"I'm certainly glad you insisted we leave our formal coats in Tucson. I believe your exact words were, 'We're cowboys, not bankers.'"

"We'll need a bath," Brannon mumbled, "and we'll need fresh clothes—or maybe we should just wash these? At least we could brush them out!"

"Now isn't this a fine sight?" Fletcher laughed. "Stuart Brannon, the terror of Yavapai County, fussing around like a schoolgirl about what to wear."

"Well," Brannon huffed, "there's no reason why we should try to look our worst, is there?"

"Of course not. It's just—"

Brannon paced back and forth under the tree. "It's not that I never dress up. I mean, I had that formal frock coat at Velvet's wedding, remember?"

"What I remember," Fletcher corrected, "is that you showed up with blood and dirt from head to foot and had to borrow the Reverend's coat."

"I just don't want to embarrass Victoria, that's all."

"Victoria? Ah, it's a beautiful woman that's driving the legendary El Brannon to such trepidation!"

"Hardly," Brannon protested. "It's just a matter of common manners and—"

"And flashing dark eyes, teasing smile, and a rather lovely figure?"

Brannon stopped pacing and stared at Fletcher. Suddenly a wide smile broke over his face. Then he coughed back a chuckle and finally unleashed a full-fledged laugh.

"This is the stupidest I've ever acted in twenty years," Brannon confessed.

"Watch out, Stuart, that's the second time you've laughed this year. Keep this up and someone will begin to suspect you're human after all!"

"I remember once when Lisa and I went to a New Year's ball at the Nash home in Prescott. Everyone was in costume."

"You went in costume?"

"Yep."

"That Lisa was a remarkable woman."

"Yep."

"Well, what did you wear?"

"A serape and a big sombrero. Mostly I just ducked my head down and sat over in the corner hoping no one would spot me."

"Did it work?"

"Until the butler mistook me for a vagrant and asked me to leave."

"Is that the sombrero that hangs by your fireplace?"

"That's the one."

"Where did you ever get such a hat?"

"It was a present from a lady in Las Cruces."

"A lady in Las Cruces?"

"Don't ask," Brannon insisted. "It's a long and rather boring story."

"Stuart, listen. Don't let this go to your head, but you look about ten years younger when you smile. You really should do it more often."

"Mr. Brannon!" Earl Howland charged across the courtyard. "Mr. Brannon, I been visitin' with Miguel. He talked to this other fella, and it seems there were two Anglos in Magdalena yesterday, trying to hire some hands to push cattle across the desert."

"They might be the ones who rustled the Pacifica herd," Brannon guessed. "Did they get any takers?"

"Only a couple of drifters from the States."

"We'll ride to Magdalena and check it out tomorrow."

"Well, now," Howland offered, "that's where I had another idea. Me and Miguel—and this Estaban who works here—want to ride into town tonight and just hang around to see what we might pick up on the streets."

"There's a fiesta tonight. A party would do you good."

"Mr. Brannon, with due respect, the only party that will do me good is the one after the wedding. I'll either sit in that bunkhouse all evenin' and pine for Miss Julie, or I can go to town and get us a head start on them rustlers."

"My word, did you ever notice how much Earl is sounding like a young Stuart Brannon?" Fletcher intoned.

"I don't know if that's a compliment or an insult. Okay, Earl, it sounds like a good idea to me. But don't make a play. And don't let anyone know we're thinking of chasing them down."

"No, sir, we'll just wait for you to come in tomorrow."

"Where will I find you?" Brannon asked.

"At La Serpiente Dorada, wherever that is."

"The Golden Snake? Sounds like a mighty elegant place."

Señora Pacifica swirled up to them as Earl turned to leave.

"Don't retreat because of me, Mr. Howland."

"No, ma'am . . . eh, Señora. I was just leavin'. My, oh my, Mr. Brannon, don't she look purdier than a cactus flower on a green hill in spring? You sure do make me miss my Julie." Earl blushed.

"Mr. Brannon," she grinned as Earl hurried toward the corrals, "just how long have you kept that poor man out on the range?"

"Earl is marrying the most dangerous smile in Arizona in a few weeks. Makes a man kind of susceptible to feminine charms." Brannon strolled with her toward one of the wooden benches that circled a small oak tree.

"Well, he should be happy then. It is an exciting time. I was sixteen when I married Don Rinaldo, but I remember it well."

"My Lisa was eighteen. Did I ever tell you about—"

"Miss Reed related your tragedy when we visited at Prescott last year." Her smile dropped. "How is Miss Harriet Reed? She seemed to be a very delightful, intelligent lady."

"Harriet's a jewel in a rugged land. She's a very good friend. She should captivate the party-goers at Buckingham Palace."

"England? Is she going to England?"

"Someday she will. The way Fletcher keeps finding reasons to go to Prescott makes me a bit suspicious."

Señora Pacifica looked surprised. "A year ago I would have sworn that it was Stuart Brannon she had her eyes on."

Brannon pulled off his hat and held it in his hand. "It's hard to explain the pain of the past to someone else."

"I believe, Mr. Brannon, we may both have tasted the bitterest of all cups."

Brannon nodded slowly. "There are many heartaches on this earth. Some of them we create for ourselves. Some of them are inflicted on us by others. And some . . . well, some of them are only for the Lord to decide their origin."

"Yes, and there are many joys here, too. Don Rinaldo and I were very happy during our twelve years of marriage."

"I presume you have children."

Señora Pacifica lowered her head.

Brannon stumbled in his speech to apologize, "I'm sorry if I—"

"No, that is fine. I'm afraid the Almighty felt it better that I did not bear children. There were several miscarriages."

She raised her head and appraised the busyness of the fiesta preparations. "They are my family. Fifty-three people live here . . . at the moment. Every woman is my sister; every man is my brother; every little one is my child. I'm not being melodramatic . . . nor patronizing. They are my life. Sometimes in the tears of the night, I believe God has shown that my purpose in life is to provide for these special families.

"Now," she sighed, "I will stop talking. I don't expect you to understand my simple Latin heart."

"I do understand. People are worth living for . . . aren't they?"

"And worth dying for. What is your divine purpose, Mr. Brannon?"

Brannon sat in silence for several moments.

She waited.

"I've been doing a little searching for that myself. A man has to have more purpose than shooting men that need to be shot."

"Yes, it is a beautiful, harsh land . . . but the Lord has been gentle with me. Now, enough of that. We must prepare for the fiesta. Do you know that this is the first time I have put off the black? This yellow dress was Don Rinaldo's favorite."

"It's beautiful . . . but Earl beat me to the praise. Your Don Rinaldo had excellent taste. I wish I'd known him better."

"You would have been good friends. As we rode home from Arizona last year, he said, 'That Brannon, he is the kind of man who makes you forget there is a border between our countries.' No more, no more," she chided herself. "Felicia tells me I must talk about something besides the past."

"It is pleasant, however," Brannon added, "to have a conversation with one who also lives in the past."

"Yes, now . . . would you like to wash up? Let me show you to your room."

"What I'd like is a hot bath and my Sunday clothes that I left in Tucson," Brannon admitted. "I really feel rather wild and woolly, not being able to dress proper for your party."

"You do not need to change for my benefit. But I will tell Juan to warm some bath water for you and Mr. Fletcher. I have many of Don Rinaldo's clothes in a trunk, so please, both of you, help yourselves."

"No, Señora, I—"

"Do you think it will ever be possible for you to call me Victoria?"

"Victoria, I couldn't wear Don Rinaldo's things. It wouldn't be—"

"Stuart, what did you do with your wife's dresses?"

"I kept them right there in the closet for a long time and then put them in a trunk."

"Is that where they are now?"

"Well, no . . . I, eh, gave them to Miss Julie, Harriet, and her sister, Mrs. Barton."

"Do you regret that decision?"

"Well, no, but—"

"And I will not regret your wearing my husband's clothes. However, I must warn you. We have many guests coming to the ranch tonight to meet El Brannon. I am afraid they will be disappointed if they find you dressed as El Patron."

"Well, I can at least brush things off a bit and hang my gun on the wall."

"Yes, use the brush . . . but by no means hang your gun. The revolver is at the heart of the El Brannon legend."

The big house at Rancho Pacifica stood in the exact center of the compound. Its U-shape framed a small courtyard separate from the other buildings. The huge front doors remained open most of the time, giving the living room an open-air feeling.

A massive rock fireplace and hearth lined the back wall of the room Brannon estimated to be one hundred feet long and fifty feet wide. It served as living room, dining room, and general meeting place. The floor of the entire house was covered by large, red tile squares, and the rooms held a bounty of leather and oak furniture.

The two wings to the sides contained bedrooms. A suite of rooms on the north belonged to Señora Pacifica and Felicia, her maid and confidante. The rooms on the south were reserved for personal staff and guests.

The kitchen was a separate building straight behind the big house. Between those two buildings spread a huge, lattice-canopied patio which housed many tables for daily meals.

Most of the other homes were flat-roofed adobe structures backed up against the thick outer wall. The entire facility reminded Brannon more of a village than a ranch.

Fletcher left the bedroom wearing a black, waist-length jacket with silver trim, his hair slicked back, and his face clean-shaven, except for his mustache.

He motioned to Brannon. "Your turn, cowboy."

"And where are you headed?"

"I understand some ranking politicians from Mexico City will be here, and I have a matter of some international significance to discuss with them."

"Can't you leave all of that to Queen Victoria?"

"Now, now," Fletcher bowed, "no disparagement on Her Majesty." He turned at the doorway and looked back at Brannon. "I suppose now we each have a Victoria . . . don't we?"

Brannon poured another steaming pitcher of water into the tub. He slipped down into the relaxing wetness and leaned his head against the upright back of the tub. Closing his eyes, he thought of Victoria and the bright yellow silk dress with black lace trim.

A big, yellow flower tucked into that handsome dark hair would certainly be a heart-stopper. She's changed since last year. 'Course then I only saw her as another man's wife. I guess she still is another man's wife . . . she's older. Not old, but mature . . . eh, hardened. No, she's just had a rough year. It begins to show right around the eyes first.

After his bath and shave, Brannon sorted through the clothes, selected a clean white shirt that felt smooth and slick, and pulled on his duckings. After brushing the trousers and vest, he withdrew a fresh red bandanna from his stash, tied it about his neck, and glanced in the tiny mirror by the door post.

I don't suppose this bandanna will clash with her dress.

That dress was made for dancin'.

Dance!

Oh, no . . . not dance!

I can't dance. That's all there is to it. I won't do it. I danced for Lisa . . . once. And I'll dance for Julie, because I promised.

*But that's it. These people are natural dancers. I'd look like a
wounded bear out there.*

"Sorry, Victoria, I'm carrying a bullet from an old wound and
just can't . . .

"Please forgive me, but I promised my dear departed wife that
I would never dance with another . . .

Yeah, Lisa, you're gettin' a kick out of this, aren't ya?

He walked over to his saddlebags and searched for the locket
with Lisa's picture. He forced his hand to the bottom of the bag
and felt the cool gold locket and its soft chain trickle through his
fingers. Then suddenly he dropped the locket and left it where it
lay. Shooting one last glance in the mirror, he was surprised that
he didn't look as tired as he normally did.

*Okay, El Brannon, smile. Act like you understand what
they're saying, and don't wipe your mouth on your sleeve.*

Stuart Brannon stood amazed by the expanse of the fiesta getting underway in the spacious grounds of Rancho Pacifica.

*Four hours ago they didn't know we were going to show up,
and now people are rolling in from miles away. A piñata? They
didn't have time to make a piñata, did they? And the musicians.
Do they work here? Are they on call? Lisa planned a party
months in advance. But this is better. Always keep a party only
a few hours away. I could buy some piñatas in Tucson and just
keep them at the ranch . . . and perhaps a—*

"You look handsome in that shirt."

He turned to see Victoria Pacifica approaching from the other
side of the vast living room.

"Then credit the shirt. I suppose it was one of Don Rinaldo's
favorites."

"Actually, he hated it. I bought it for him in San Francisco, but
he seldom wore it. 'I am El Patron,' he would insist, 'I cannot
wear the shirt of a riverboat gambler.'"

"I like it," Brannon declared.

"So do I. It is yours; please keep it."

"Oh, no . . . I didn't mean to—"

"Stuart, here is your first lesson in hacienda hospitality: It is a grave insult to refuse a gift."

"Victoria," he said with his head tilted slightly, "thank you for the shirt. Now may I ask you another question of etiquette?"

"Most certainly."

"Well, with this room half-opened up and all, is it acceptable for me to keep my hat on?"

"Of course. But tell me, why do you look so nervous?"

"I suppose that's the effect beautiful women have on me."

"You, too, have been on the trail much too long. Come. Let me introduce you to my friends."

She slipped her arm in Brannon's and led him out into the courtyard.

"Would you rather I introduced you in Spanish or in English?"

"Do they all speak English?"

"No, but many would like to."

"Let's make it English then. I won't be so self-conscious about my grammar."

"Your grammar is very respectable. Did you learn your Spanish in Mexico?"

"No, in south Texas."

"Ah, that is close enough."

"And where did you learn your English?"

"In St. Louis."

"What were you doing in St. Louis?"

"Going to school. But that's a long story I'll tell you another time."

Brannon stopped their stroll and looked her in the eyes. "Have you noticed that both of us seem to have many long stories from the past that we plan on explaining to each other at some future time?"

"Yes, I believe you are right."

"Do you ever think we'll be together long enough to tell all those stories?"

"I am counting on it, Stuart Brannon. I am counting on it," she answered softly, almost without moving her lips, as the first guest approached them.

For the next hour and twenty minutes Brannon shook hands with every man, woman, boy, and girl at the fiesta. Some more than once.

It was well after dark when one of the workers approached Señora Pacifica and announced that the food was ready. A loud bell clanged and echoed throughout the hacienda. Everyone gathered by the great oak. Then the lady of the house took control. With Brannon's aid she stepped up on a bench and addressed the crowd.

"*Tienen que comprender, Don Rinaldo y yo* . . . were some of many people whom El Brannon has rescued over the years. He is a man of valor and integrity, and it is my pleasure to introduce him as a good friend. Please help yourselves to all the food that has been prepared by my most excellent staff. But first, our guest, Mr. Stuart Brannon of Yavapai County, Arizona . . . *dira la benedición.*"

Everyone waited, perfectly still, staring at Brannon.

"Did you ask me to say a blessing?" he whispered.

"Yes, but if you are too uncomfortable, I could—"

"Ah . . . well, no . . . I'll do it. It's just—"

"In Spanish, if you don't mind."

Brannon cleared his throat, searched for a friendly face, and found that all—even Fletcher's—bowed downward.

"*El Señor. La tierra en la frontera, en los Estados Unidos y aquí en Mexico es un lugar hermoso y espacioso* . . . Thanks for allowing us the joy of living on it. But, Lord, You know it can be a harsh and unforgiving place as well. So help us to meet our trials with tolerance, our failures with confession and patience, and our enemies with justice and mercy. We ask Your strength from this wonderful food and Your blessing on those who have gathered here. May You continue to give Señora Pacifica your wisdom as she oversees . . . *esta hacienda. En el nombre de Jesús. Amén.*"

At once the entire crowd swarmed to the patio behind the big house. Brannon, ready to be swept along, felt a woman's warm hand clutching his and holding him back.

Victoria Pacifica smiled at the others who were leaving, but did not release Brannon. Not until the last guest was out of earshot did she ease her grasp.

"I owe you an apology, and I must make a confession."

"About the prayer?"

"Yes. It was improper to ask you in front of the others. I had no right to do that, and I beg your forgiveness."

"It's all right. You just surprised me. Not many people have ever asked Stuart Brannon to pray."

"It is their loss. However, there is also a confession." She sighed deeply and looked away. "I purposely manipulated you into that position. It is not something that I often do—and I deeply regret it. It is just that I wanted very much to hear you pray."

"Why was that?"

"Because I believe prayer, especially prayer under pressure, quickly reveals more about a man than anything else he can do."

"So you were testing me?"

"Yes. And you certainly would be justified to retaliate."

"Did I pass the test?"

"Someday when we have more time, I will tell you how well you did."

"That is a promise that I will make you keep." He took her arm and led her toward the tables of food.

"Many will want to talk to you now," Victoria said, "so I will oversee the serving." She slipped from his grasp. "Remember, the guest of honor is required to have the first dance with the hostess."

"Dance?" Brannon groaned. "No, I can't. Actually it's—"

She disappeared into the crowd.

"I say, Brannon," Fletcher said merrily, "that was a lovely prayer. Mexico is a magical place where even famous gunmen pray."

"Well, Edwin, I hope there will be no more surprises tonight."

"Do you want a real surprise? Do you see that tall fellow over there, the one with the narrow-brimmed hat? He is not Mexican, but, in fact, a Hebrew. And he has a fascinating story about how some of his people are planning to reclaim Palestine for the Jews. Now wouldn't that be an interesting idea?"

"I wonder if anyone has told the Turks?"

"My word, that's a good point. Think I'll go back and have another chat."

Brannon determined to try a little of everything on the food tables, but one glance and he realized it would be impossible. He settled for a plate piled full of tortillas, roast pork, chili peppers, and fresh fruit.

To his relief, he found that most of the guests enjoyed eating even more than talking with El Brannon. He savored the meal with only occasional interruptions.

I knew this was going to happen. I've said it before—I am not a dancer. I'd do almost anything not to offend the Señora, but straight out . . . I will not dance. I'll fall down, hurt myself, hurt her. There is absolutely no way.

"There you are. Still eating?"

He turned to see Victoria Pacifica.

"About that dance . . . ," he began.

"Oh, yes, let me explain. You will put your right hand on my left shoulder. When the music begins we will sidestep three times to your left. Then we will twirl around once, and repeat. That's all there is to it: three steps, twirl, three steps twirl, and so on. We will go around the outside of the front courtyard one time . . . and then you may sit down. Your chores will be over. At that time you truly may decline, and I will not be offended."

Before he answered she turned her gaze upward at the stars. "It is, is it not, a beautiful night for dancing?"

"Eh, yes . . . it's a beautiful night."

"Will you dance the first dance with me?"

Brannon cleared his throat. "I'd be delighted."

"Thank you for consenting," she grinned, "but you do not lie very well."

"I do not dance well either," he confided.

Brannon found the pace and confusion of the dancing so hectic that it was over before he had much time to worry. Fortunately for him, the men wanted to talk to El Brannon more than the women wanted to dance. He spent most of the evening discussing the finer points of the cattle business, gold mines in Colorado, and the best people to talk to in Washington, D.C.—if one had a legitimate land grant claim in the territories.

As he had expected, about midnight the band members began to gather their things. The party obviously was winding down. Then to Brannon's amazement another band entered and began to play livelier music, and more loudly, than the first.

It was close to dawn when the last guest's carriage rolled out of the yard and the staff began to put things away. The night had been cool, but never cold. Brannon sat on the large leather couch in the living room holding a cup of coffee in a thick pottery mug.

"You toss a fine party, ma'am." He leaned back on the couch and closed his eyes as Señora Pacifica sat down in a chair across from him.

"Why thank you, sir. And you make a very delightful guest of honor."

"Oh?"

"Yes, six different ladies asked me privately if you were married. Two of them are already engaged . . . and one is married!"

"It must be the shirt," he chuckled.

She tucked her feet up under her and began to laugh. She looked at Brannon and started to say something, then laughed again.

"No, no," she finally blurted out. "It was not the shirt. I believe it was the poor lighting."

Brannon felt laughter burst loose from deep within himself. Rolling, uncontrollable, long-suppressed laughter. Finally, when they settled down a bit, she continued.

"Mr. Brannon, you are not nearly as somber a man as you would like others to believe."

He took a deep sigh. "It feels sort of good to laugh, doesn't it?"

"The death of a mate teaches one much about crying, but very little about laughter."

The sound of hoofbeats and shouts from the front gate of the hacienda propelled both Pacifica and Brannon out of their chairs and into the yard.

Jumping from his horse, Estaban ran to them.

"Señora . . . it is bad . . . very bad . . . in Magdalena . . . they shot them!"

"Who got shot?" Brannon demanded.

"Miguel y Señor Howland!"

"Are they dead?"

"Miguel was wounded in the side and was taken to the house of his *tia*."

"And Earl! What about Earl?" Brannon begged.

"They shot him in the leg and then took him away!"

"Who shot him? Who took him?"

"Captain Porter."

"Porter?"

"Yes, it was Porter himself!"

"Where did they take him?"

"I do not know, I do not know. I raced back here as fast as the horse would run!"

"Estaban, grab something to eat. Then throw your saddle on another mount. I'll need you to ride back with us."

"Victoria, have your cook make several grub sacks . . . we'll need to borrow some supplies. I'll roust out Edwin, Jaime, and Mateo."

"You must leave immediately?"

"Yep."

"Ramon will be here soon. I can send him and some others."

"We'd appreciate the help. I don't know what we're facing. They can catch up with us in Magdalena. But please, keep enough men here to make the hacienda safe."

"Remember we have many long conversations to finish," she insisted.

"I won't forget."

"Nor will I. May God be with you, Stuart Brannon."

"And with you, Victoria Pacifica."

FIVE

El Viento sweated white foam and labored for each breath as the party finally entered Magdalena.

Brannon was tired.

Tired from no sleep.

Tired from a hard ride.

And especially tired from the mental thrashing he'd given himself during three long hours in the saddle.

Sure, go to the fiesta . . . eat the fine meal . . . listen to the music . . . dance with the women . . . visit with Victoria . . . while Earl's in town doing your job. Lord, I can't believe I did this! How do I explain this to Miss Julie? How do I explain this to myself? If Earl dies . . . I'll . . . I'll marry Miss Julie myself.

"I say, Brannon, what is this, a festival? I've never seen a city so packed with people—except in India, of course," Fletcher offered as they wound their way through the crowded streets.

"I presume it's market day, right, Esteban?" Brannon kept El Viento moving through the throngs of people.

"Yes, Señor . . . the Saturday before the first Sunday of every month. For many, it is their only trip to town."

The marketplace stretching out in front of the gigantic church was packed with buyers and sellers. The scene spilled into every street, every alley, every corner, and every vacant lot. Animals, milk products, bread, fresh fruit, vegetables, meat, tortillas, cloth, dresses, hats, shoes, leather products, packaged goods from the States, guns, knives, liquor, and religious statues piled the stands. Everyone seemed to laugh, shout, cry, and threaten their way through every transaction.

As Brannon had imagined, La Serpiente Dorada was located in the worst part of the city, on a street lined with broken-down cantinas sporting names such as La Cabeza de Vaca, El Cubo de Sangre, Santa Anna's Venganza, and Tia Maria Gorda.

Leaving Jaime in the street to watch the horses, Brannon, Fletcher, Estaban, and Mateo entered La Serpiente Dorada.

The saloon reeked with stale smoke, shouts and curses, and patrons. Drunk, sober, male, female, Mexican and Anglo patrons—each seemed to be carrying a drink and a grudge. Six bartenders manned the long bar. The one least busy looked American. Brannon approached him.

"I hear there was a shooting in here last night."

The man shrugged and then answered in English, "There are shootin's in here every night."

"Well, a friend of mine might have gotten shot last night. I'm trying to find him to make sure he's all right."

"Look, I ain't got no idea who got shot or where they are now."

"Perhaps someone else knows," Fletcher probed.

"Maybe. Maybe not."

Brannon shifted weight from one foot to the other and tugged his hat down.

"He might be with a Captain Porter or his men. Can you tell me where I might find them?"

The man glanced around the bar and then back at Brannon. "Look, you want to buy a drink or not?"

"All I want is a simple answer, and then I'll get out of your fine establishment," Brannon growled. "Where did they take my friend?"

Suddenly the bartender whipped a short-barrel scatter gun from behind the bar and laid it on the counter with the barrel aimed at Brannon's stomach.

"Look, Mister," he snarled, "order a drink, or beat it. I wouldn't tell any man in this town . . . " He turned and casually launched a spurt of tobacco juice toward a spittoon. "Shoot, I wouldn't even tell old Stuart Brannon himself where Porter is. I ain't that stupid. Now get out of here or there'll be another shootin'!"

Estaban crowded in and glared at the bartender. "You just might get that chance to face El Brannon."

"What?"

Brannon nodded toward the far end of the bar. "See that man at the end?"

The bartender glanced away. "Is he Brannon?" he muttered. Brannon grabbed the barrel of the scattergun, slammed the butt of the stock into the big man's stomach, seized the lapel of his vest and thrust the man's head into the whiskey-stained bar. Brannon whipped his Colt from its holster and laid it aside the man's temple.

Brannon leaned to the man's ear and whispered, "He's not Brannon—I am!"

"Y-y-you ain't Brannon," the man stuttered. "H-h-he's taller and bigger."

The hammer on Brannon's revolver clicked back.

"Look, Mister, whoever you are . . . I cain't tell where Porter is. I don't know . . . honest. They don't tell nobody."

"You know," Brannon sneered, "it's sort of sad when a man's last words on earth are a lie." He exaggerated the movement of his trigger finger.

"Wait!" the big man sweated out an answer. "It's out west of town, toward the desert . . . up on a mesa. That's all I know."

"Why did they haul my friend off?"

"Porter's been tryin' to hire hands to drive some cattle, but no one wants to sign on."

"Why's that?"

"'Cause he's crazy, that's why. Once you hitch up with Porter you either stay with him or you disappear."

"Disappear?"

"Yeah. He's a tough guy to walk away from . . . if you get the drift."

"So he's taken to shooting and kidnapping hired hands?"

"I guess your friend refused to volunteer."

Brannon released the man and lowered the Colt. The bartender rubbed his jaw and glanced down the bar again.

"Say, is that really Brannon down there?"

"Good heavens, no," Fletcher insisted. "Stuart Brannon is seven feet tall!"

"I knew that," the bartender grumbled. "That's exactly what I tried to tell ya."

Suddenly they heard shouts in the street in front of the saloon. Brannon ran for the door. Outside he saw a man holding a gun on Jaime. Brannon drew his own, but felt the hard steel of a pistol barrel shoved against his back.

"Well, well, well . . . if it isn't Tres Casa's most famous lawman. This time I have the upper hand."

"Ramon?"

"You remember . . . I'm flattered. Do you remember the humiliation of that day?"

"It was years ago. You were drunk and running with bad company."

People began drifting out of the cantinas to watch the confrontation.

"I remember every detail. And now I have the drop."

"Look, Ramon, I'm trying to find a friend so we can go and retrieve that herd of cattle for you and your sister. We're on the same side this time."

"I can find the cattle on my own."

"Sure, anyone can find the trail of 850 head. But can you take them away from Porter and his army of outlaws?"

"We do not need you, Stuart Brannon. You will be riding back to Arizona."

"I don't think so, Ramon. Listen, ask Estaban. We are in this thing together."

"He is correct, Señor Ramon. Mr. Brannon has been very helpful to the Señora."

"Take your boots off, Brannon!" Ramon shouted as the crowd grew in size.

"Good heavens, Stuart." Fletcher questioned, "Do you want us to—"

"The man has the gun in my back so I had better do what he says."

Brannon bent down and lifted a leg of his trousers, but instead of tugging on the boot he slipped his knife out of its sheath. He swung it up briskly, lightly slicing the back of Ramon's hand.

Ramon dropped the revolver, and Brannon yanked Ramon's hat which had been hanging by the stampede string on his back. Brannon whipped his knife to the challenger's neck and shouted to the accomplices in the street.

"*¡Pistoleros los cañones!*"

Jaime retrieved his own revolver and shouted to the crowd, "*¡Este es El Brannon!*"

The crowd murmured, "*¿El Brannon? ¿En Magdalena?*"

"You might as well slit my throat," Ramon rasped under his breath. "You have humiliated me for the last time. This is my home. I will be laughed at forever."

Brannon continued to pin Ramon with the knife, and whispered, "Do exactly what I say and you can still be a hero. When I let you go, laugh your hardest and throw your arms around me."

"*¿Qué?*"

Brannon suddenly released Ramon, grabbed him by the shoulder, and laughed.

"*¡Ramon! ¡Mi buen amigo! ¡Siempre hace travesuras!*"

At first startled, then with fresh brightness in his eyes, Ramon began to laugh. Brannon picked up Ramon's gun, handed it to him, and then threw his arm around the young man's shoulder.

"*¿Dígame, cómo está su hermana hermosa, la Señora Pacifica?*"

Ramon, now sensing the crowd's amazement, widened his smile.

"*Ah, ella se lamenta por Don Rinaldo, y quiere ver al buen amigo de nuestra familia, Señor Stuart Brannon.*"

Brannon turned to the crowd. "*Amigos, ¿sabían que este hombre, Ramon, es el segundo luchador en Tres Casas, New Mexico? ¡Soy el mas superior, por supuesto!*"

The cantina patrons laughed hard and then began to disperse, shaking their heads.

"*¿Ramon y El Brannon?*"

"No one but a good friend could play such a joke on El Brannon and live."

"That is our Ramon. I have known him since he was a boy!"

Brannon and his partners ambled toward their horses.

"We have not completely settled the matter," Ramon complained. "But thank you for allowing me to preserve my honor."

"Did the authorities send troops?"

"There are no authorities."

"Your uncle in Monterrey?"

"He has been arrested and is bound for Mexico City."

"And the Federales?"

"They are fighting a revolution of some sort."

"So there's no help?"

Ramon wrapped a black bandanna around his wounded hand. "Only us."

"Look, Ramon. Let's make a truce. I've got to find Earl Howland, and we've both got to retrieve a herd of cattle. How about working together for a while?"

Ramon squeezed his bleeding hand. "I'll agree to that."

"How many men did you bring with you?"

"Three. It's all we have who can use a gun well."

"Hopefully that will be enough."

"Where are we going now?"

"To find a mesa west of town."

"The tracks show the herd was driven south."

Brannon mounted El Viento and then slowly rubbed the back of his neck. "I had assumed Porter drove the cattle right to his place, but that might not be the case. Listen, Ramon, take your men, plus Jaime and Mateo, and follow the trail of the cattle. But hang back, and don't get too close. Find out where they're kept. We'll catch up with you as soon as Earl is free. We need to know ahead of time how many fighting men Porter has with the herd."

"You will go to the mesa?"

"Yes, I'll take Fletcher with me."

Estaban rode over to Brannon. "I will go to the mesa with you."

"No, you need to rest. Go back to the *rancho* and tell the Señora what we are doing. Is there any quick way out of this city?"

"Ride straight north on this street and then circle around to the west," Ramon advised. "When should we expect you?"

"In three days at the most," Brannon replied.

Pushing their way through the bartering crowd, Brannon and Fletcher rode north.

The air was dry . . . but not hot, and the dust from the street was hardly noticeable. Brannon rolled the sleeves of his white shirt halfway up his forearms. In the stream of people approaching Magdalena at the north entrance he noticed three Anglos riding tired Texas ponies.

Brannon pulled his hat down, planning to ride by, but one called out.

"Excuse me, partner! You, on that big black—you're American, ain't ya?"

Brannon glanced up. "What can I do for you, stranger?"

"Listen, we ain't never been down in this part of Mexico before. And we's lookin' for La Serpantia Dorader. Got to meet a fella there, but I ain't got no idea where it is."

"You wouldn't be looking for Captain Porter, would you?"

The man broke into a smile. "Yes, sir, we are! Hear he's hirin' on, and we need a little job south of the border for a while . . . you know what I mean? Anyway, we're carrying this letter of approval from Colonel H. B. Johnson himself."

"Letter of approval?"

"Well, yep. Ain't jist anybody who can hire on with Porter. You have to have a letter of approval from a Confederate officer, you know. Been carrying this letter for ten years, jist in case I needed it."

"I didn't know that. I think maybe recruitment has slacked off since you got that letter. He seems to be rounding up just about anybody."

"Why, was you going to sign on yourself?"

Brannon began to circle the city with the others riding along. "We aim to talk to him."

"Then you know where he is?"

"Yep."

"You headin' there now?"

"Yep."

"Mind if we tag along?"

"Be my guests."

"This is our lucky day, boys. We don't have to waste time in the city. Say, listen, this here letter recommends six of us from North Carolina, but three of us took some lead up in Arizona. Two dead and the other shot up bad. If ya want to, you can jist pretend like you are two of those other boys!"

Brannon kept a stern face. "That's mighty thoughtful of you. How'd your friends get shot?"

"They was cold-blooded murdered by that outlaw named Stryker Banyon!"

Fletcher offered, "You don't mean that Stuart Brannon chap?"

"That's the one! They was on the train just goin' about their business."

"And he shot them point blank?" Brannon asked.

"Well, no sir. I guess they was, you know, robbing the train, but they hardly ever do anything mean enough to shoot."

"Say, wasn't that the famous Matee gang?" Brannon asked.

"Why, that's us! What's left of us. I'm Cletus Matee, and them is my cousins, Taft and Tater."

"Howdy, boys." Brannon tipped his hat.

"Say, I don't remember your name."

"Well," Brannon began, "most around here call me El Viejo."

"El Viejo? The old man? Shoot, you don't look much over forty."

"You know how they are on a cattle drive. I was the boss, so I'm called The Old Man."

This time it was Tater that spoke up. "Yeah, but what was your name in the States?"

"Tater!" Cletus Matee scolded. "Don't you ever ask that. We ain't in Carolina now. It don't matter what a man used to be called. No, sir. Sorry about that, El Viejo. These boys are new to the West and they jist ain't learned yet."

"No problem."

Looking at Fletcher, Matee quizzed, "How about you, furiner? What do you want us to call ya?"

"Ed," Brannon interjected. "Just call him Ed."

"Ed?" Fletcher choked, but Brannon silenced him with a curt nod.

Little more was said until they had partially circled Magdalena and started to ride an increasingly dusty road toward the west. Brannon and Fletcher rode together, then Cletus, with Taft and Tater bringing up the rear.

Fletcher stretched out an arm. "I presume that's the mesa out there?"

"It's the only one in this direction."

"You can't sneak up on it," Fletcher said softly. "What's the plan?"

"Just ride in there with these old boys, I suppose."

"Even El Viejo wouldn't stand a chance with thirty men in their own lair."

"We'll do all right until someone figures out who we are. Sounds to me like the number of men has dwindled. As far as I understand, no one knows who I am."

"What about Rube Woolsey, the man at the well? If he's with Porter, he'll spot you."

"You're right about that. I hadn't thought about him. Anyway, they must have split the gang and sent some off with the cattle. Maybe he's on that detail."

Fletcher glanced around to see Cletus lagging back to converse with his cousins. "And maybe someone else will recognize the legendary Stuart Brannon."

"You know," Brannon continued, "the only good thing about those Hawthorne Miller books is that they're so exaggerated no one would ever figure out it was me."

"How far away do you think they can see us?"

"Up on the mesa?"

"Yes."

"I expect a good spyglass could pick us up now."

Cletus came riding up. "Say, El Viejo, where did you get that horse? He sure is a beauty."

"His name is El Viento, and he's faster than the wind. A lady up in Colorado gave him to me."

"Say, a ladies' man, huh? Look, we don't speak none of this here Mexican. Maybe you could introduce us to a few ladies."

"If the opportunity presents itself, I'll do that."

"Listen, Tater heard that Porter will pay us three dollars a day and expenses. Is that what you heard?"

"Sounds good to me."

"Yes, sir, it does. We been kind of thinkin' about gettin' out of the outlaw business. After a while you get tired of hidin' in the rocks."

"If you don't mind me asking," Fletcher said, "how long have you men been doing this?"

"What's it been, Taft? Two? Three? Four? About five months, I guess."

The shortest of the three, Taft, rubbed his six-day beard and spoke. "Five months and three days since we pulled that job in Poplar Gulch, Arkansas."

"Well, boys, a little cattle drive ought to do you good."

"Yep, that's what I been tellin' 'em."

The road had stretched in a straight line for ten miles. Now it began a very slow ascent and turned to the south as the men nooned from the back of the saddle. The sun was halfway down the sky as they reached the base of the mesa.

"Okay, Old Man, where do we go from here?"

"Unless I'm wrong, I expect a greeting party to come out and meet us. Cletus, you're packing that letter of approval. How about you leading and doing the talking?"

"Yep, I will. Look up there. The trail branches off and goes through that narrow rock canyon. Is that the right way?"

"I could almost bank on it."

Without saying anything else, Brannon dropped back behind the others. He pulled his Winchester out of the scabbard and laid it across the saddle as he rode.

"Is this where we make the play?" Fletcher asked softly.

"I hope not. We haven't found Earl yet. But who knows?"

In a matter of moments, two riders appeared, trotting straight down the narrow trail at them. Brannon spotted two more men in the rocks on the high side of the mesa. With hat pulled low and hand still on the rifle, he listened to the conversation.

"I'm afraid you boys are on the wrong trail," one of the men explained. "This is a private road. You'll have to turn around."

"We ain't lookin' for no trouble," Cletus offered. "But we were looking for Captain Porter. We got a letter of approval here from Col. H. B. Johnson himself."

"A letter of approval? You boys from the South?"

"I didn't learn to talk this way in New York City," Cletus drawled.

After looking at the letter, the spokesman waved off the gun-men on the mesa.

"Glad to see you boys. We haven't had any volunteers in over a year! Ain't many of us left, so we just sort of drafted some, if you know what I mean."

"Drafted?" Cletus asked.

"Oh, we pulled a few out of town and put them to work punching cattle."

"Mexicans?"

"Nope. You can't trust 'em. No Mexicans, Indians, or Yankees allowed."

Brannon winked at Fletcher.

"I'll lead you boys on up. Captain Porter will be mighty pleased to see you."

The trail was so narrow they climbed to the top riding single file.

Easy to defend . . . and easy to get trapped. Sort of like Masada. This trail would be a tad spooky in the dark. They probably stake a couple guards at the bottom all night. Lord, these men are just organized outlaws and murderers . . . and someone ought to do something about them. But I'd rather it not be me. I just want to find Earl and get him out of here.

The top of the mesa sloped gently to the south, and Brannon reckoned it to be about a mile long and a half mile wide. There were only a few scraggly trees, and the ground was covered with ankle-deep grass. At the head of the trail lay a small, fort-like compound that consisted of three modest adobe buildings fac-ing each other around a small courtyard. A stout shoulder-high adobe wall closed in the open side of the courtyard.

There seemed to be no corrals, and horses grazed all along the top of the mesa. Brannon could spot no more than a half-dozen men, who all stopped what they were doing to watch the new group come in.

Brannon hung back, letting Cletus do all the talking, and searched for traces of Earl Howland.

If he's up here, he's in one of those three little buildings. But which one?

A man with a commanding presence and a faded Confederate hat emerged from the center building and, after scanning the letter of approval, greeted the newcomers. Brannon figured the man was an inch or two taller than himself. He was clean-shaven and packed at least two revolvers. The man sized up the newly arrived crew.

"You boys can bunk over in that house. Some of the men are out with the herd, so we have extra room. You made it just in time though. One day later and we would have pulled shuck.

"You're in the army, boys. You'll help in the liberation of Baja. And you get to divide up the spoils when we sell the cattle. The conscripts will drive herd. You're needed mainly for your guns. Now eat some supper. It will be the last meal we have before we hit the trail."

While he filled up his soiled tin plate with a gray lumpy stew, Brannon chatted with the cook.

"Isn't that old boy over in the chair going to eat?" he asked.

"Lee Don? He's a guardin' the conscripts. He eats later."

"How many of them shanghaied cowboys are in there?"

"One."

"Only one?"

"The others are out with the herd, but that one's a hard case. I don't figure he'll ride with us, if you get the drift."

Brannon grabbed a hunk of bread that felt hard as stone and wandered across the dirt courtyard to the man in the chair who was gazing at the food.

"Are you Lee Don?"

"Yep," the big man answered.

"Well, you should get some grub. Captain Porter says to eat hearty. We'll be on the trail soon."

"You one of those new men who just rode in?"

"Yep."

"You're going to take my turn on guard?"

"Yep. Any special instructions?"

"Sure," Lee Don grinned, revealing a deficit of front teeth. "If he tries anything, shoot him."

"Am I supposed to feed him?"

"Don't matter to me. He probably ain't going to be around long enough to digest it anyways." Lee Don wandered back across the yard and took his place at the dinner table.

Brannon pushed the rough, worn wooden door open just a crack and sat down at the chair facing the yard. He glanced at Fletcher who had taken the horses out to the mesa and was loosening the saddles.

With a wad of bitter, salty stew crammed in his cheek, he spoke in a hushed tone. "Earl?"

"Is that you, Mr. Brannon?"

"Yep. How bad you shot?"

"Just caught the back of my leg. It stopped bleedin', but it burns like the dickens!"

"Can you walk?"

"I could, but they got me roped to a chair. What's the plan, Mr. Brannon?"

"Wait 'til night, I suppose."

"Who's with ya?"

"Just me and Fletcher."

"How'd you get up here without a gunfight?"

"They think I'm joining the cause."

"Watch your step. They'll shoot ya for sure if they think you're crossin' 'em."

"Earl, I'm going to close the door. I think Porter is heading this way."

Two men carrying shotguns followed directly behind Porter as he approached.

"You one of the new men with Cletus?" Porter asked.

"Yep."

"You think you got what it takes to be in this outfit?"

"Yep."

"Well, we got a traitor in our midst. There's a man in that room who refuses to assist us."

"A man of narrow vision, no doubt."

"My sentiments exactly," Porter smiled. "Now go in there and shoot him. We might as well find out about you right now."

Brannon stood and looked Porter in the eyes. "I hate to waste a bullet. Couldn't we just hang him or throw him over the side of a cliff?"

"I can guarantee you we have plenty of bullets."

"That's good enough for me."

Brannon pushed into the room and swung the door closed behind him.

SIX

arl," Brannon whispered, "I'm going to pretend to shoot ya, and you've got to play dead." He held his revolver about a foot above the earthen floor and fired straight into the ground. Dust flew and the room smelled of gunpowder. Pulling his knife quickly, he sliced apart the ropes that bound Howland's hands and feet.

As he had hoped, the leg wound was still bloody, so Brannon smeared some of the blood on his hand and across Howland's face. He jammed on his friend's hat and quickly hefted him across his shoulders.

"Play dead," he reminded.

As he turned to the door, Porter shoved it open and stepped inside.

"What are you doing with him?"

"I figured you didn't want the body rottin' up the place, so I was going to toss this old boy over the edge of the mesa."

Brannon studied Porter.

His face is too flushed . . . his neck is too red . . . he drinks too much.

"Well . . . yes, that will be fine. Quick work like that will get you far in this outfit."

"Yes, sir. Thank ya."

Brannon had to turn sideways to get Howland through the

doorway. As he did, he scooped up his rifle that had been propped against the adobe wall.

"Hey, I don't see any mortal wound!"

Brannon glanced over to see one of Porter's henchmen pointing at Howland.

"That's why I screwed his hat down tight. It ain't a pretty sight. Kind of like scalpin' a man with dynamite. If you haven't had your supper, I wouldn't suggest lookin' at it. Do you still want to see?"

"Not me," the other henchman intoned. "Captain, I'm goin' to grab some chuck."

"Ace, you go with this man. What's your name?"

"Call me Tex."

"I thought y'all were from North Carolina?"

"Nope."

"Yeah, well, help Tex get rid of this hard case," Porter commanded.

Brannon protested, "How about me just rounding up that fellow over by the remuda? I figure I'll have to pack this body horseback anyway."

Brannon watched Porter's eyes.

Empty. Lord, there's not a scrap of mercy in that man.

"I give the orders around here," Porter snapped.

"That's fair enough, but he is gettin' heavy."

"Ace will go with you, and then report right back to me."

"Yes, sir," Brannon replied, "and can we use the horses?"

"Yeah, I don't care. Grab another man if you need to."

"You want to help me tote this old boy?" Brannon asked.

Ace pushed his hat back with the barrel of his scattergun. "I ain't carryin' no dead man."

As they approached the remuda, Brannon yelled at Fletcher who was still acting busy with horses.

"Hey, Ed! Bring a couple of them mounts over here."

Fletcher approached with El Viento and his own horse.

"And toss a hooly over that dusty chestnut. He looks stout

enough to tote a body. How come all these horses are still saddled, Ace?"

"We're ridin' out of here real soon."

Brannon tossed Howland across the saddle on his horse,
almost losing him as he slipped toward the ground. He had to
grab Howland's belt and pull him up on the saddle.

"Maybe you ought to tie him down," Ace suggested.

"What for? If he falls off, it won't hurt him."

"That's for sure. I'll get my pony."

Brannon and Fletcher were mounted as they waited for Ace
to circle around near them.

Ace looked down at Howland. "You really took the top off
his head, did ya?"

"You know," Brannon replied, "there's just not a clean way
to do it, is there?"

Ace rode his horse right next to Howland. "Well, I've seen
plum near ever'thing. He bent down so his head was only a couple feet from Howland's and then pulled off the hat.

Howland jerked up his head, face still smeared with blood,
and roared at the top of his voice.

Ace shot up and yanked back on the reins, causing his horse
to rear and bolt across the meadow. Ace plunged to the ground
as several of the men from the headquarters came running out,
guns drawn.

Brannon leaped off El Viento and bent down as if to assist the
stunned Ace. He slammed the barrel of his revolver against the
man's head.

"What happened out here?" one of the men shouted.

"Ace got bucked off. Must have hit his head on something
hard. You boys take him back to the bunk. Me and Ed will finish up with this other one." He motioned toward Howland, once
again limp on the saddle.

The men yanked Ace off the ground and packed him back to
the house. Brannon, Fletcher, and Howland rode toward the

edge of the mesa. Once out of earshot, Fletcher spoke up. "I say, Stuart, isn't the trail more to the right?"

"Yep. But I figure those at the cabin are watching us right now. I don't want to show our cards too soon."

"Mr. Brannon, I'm gettin' awful stiff," Howland complained.

"Not nearly as stiff as they had hoped."

"Are they going to let us just ride off?" Fletcher asked.

"I doubt it, but we got a lot further than I thought we would."

"Stuart, take a glance back," Fletcher nodded. "Looks like they're all heading for the ponies."

"I suppose Ace just woke up. All right, Earl, you can sit up. Let's get down off this mesa. I don't suppose there's another trail."

"Not that I know of. Mr. Brannon, have you got another revolver?"

Brannon dug in his saddlebag and handed a .45 to Howland.

"Edwin, take the lead down. It's gettin' shadowy, so watch yourself. Earl, stay in the middle. I'll drop back and slow them down a bit. We'll probably get a fight all the way down. Remember, he has two men on the side of the mesa and probably two at the bottom. They'll try to pin us down so we'll have to keep moving. Once we make it to the desert floor, we'll have a better chance."

"What will we do then?" Howland begged.

"Don't worry about that now."

"My word, Earl," Fletcher called back, "we probably won't make it that far anyway,"

Brannon could hear gunshots coming his way as he plunged El Viento down the trail leading off the mesa. About twenty feet down the mountain he reined up the big black gelding and slid out of the saddle, clutching his Winchester.

Climbing across the boulders that ascended above the head of the trail, he began to shove boulders down. But the riders already were too close, so he abandoned the avalanche and retreated to

El Viento. He returned fire at the lead horse, still too distant to do any damage, but close enough to slow the pursuers.

When he reached the trail where he had left El Viento, the big horse was gone. One glance at the tracks told Brannon the steed had trotted down to Howland and Fletcher.

"Why me?" Brannon moaned aloud. "I'm going to sell him and buy a horse that's deaf!" He began to race down the trail on foot. As he whipped around a tight horseshoe corner of the trail, several shots rang out against the rocks above his head. Then he could hear gunshots down the mountain.

Fletcher and Howland!

Brannon glanced back up the trail. The descending horsemen had gained on him. Gasping to relieve a cramp in his side, he glanced up above the trail. There on the hillside was a large, round boulder about the size of a yearling steer, hanging over the trail. Under the overhang was a small stick of wood about a foot long that seemed to be bracing the rock, keeping it from falling on the trail.

"If I can hit that stick," he said through clenched teeth, "that boulder ought to come right down!" Lifting the Winchester to his shoulder, he pulled off a quick shot.

The stick burst into splinters.

The bullet ricocheted off the rocks above.

But the big boulder stood still.

A joke? Someone put that there for a . . .

Just then the lead horse stumbled and collapsed at the turn of the narrow trail.

Who shot the horse? The ricochet? Shoot the horse . . . block the trail? Why didn't I think of that?

Ahead on the trail he could see Fletcher and Howland pinned against the steep side of the mesa with two gunmen above them and two more blocking the trail below. He began to work his way out onto the rocks above where Porter's men crouched.

Circling above them, he was just about in position to fire when two rapid shots from the trail sent him diving to the rocks.

Fletcher? It's me up here. He thinks I'm still down there!

The shots at Brannon alerted Porter's men to his presence and they whipped around, firing more shots his way.

This is great. I should always go it alone. If I raise up to shoot Porter's men, Fletcher and Howland will fire at me.

Brannon rose up just enough to fire two quick shots at the rocks next to Fletcher and Howland. They both ducked for cover as he fired two more shots at Porter's men. One of them tumbled back. The other dropped his rifle and clutched his right arm.

Just then two more shots splintered granite near Brannon. He set his black hat on the end of the rifle barrel and raised it out in the clear.

Maybe Earl and Edwin will recognize my hat.

A half-dozen shots spun the hat like a top.

Fletcher and Howland scrambled on down the trail, El Viento trotting about twenty feet behind.

I'll have to work my way back to the trail, unseen. If my enemies don't shoot me, my friends will!

Crawling among the rocks was slow and tedious, and Brannon could only bang his shins and skin his knuckles as he listened to Fletcher and Howland shooting to keep from being pinned down from both directions.

Sounds like they got that horse drug off.

Suddenly the side of the mesa ahead of Brannon broke out of the rocks, and there was a steep red dirt decline in front of him. In the distance the sun glowed against the Sierra Madres. Magdalena was only a dark blotch on the horizon.

Brannon took a quick glance at the steep descent, then plunged feet-first down the mountain. A few steps later he lost his balance and tumbled into the red clay. Tightly clutching his Winchester, he somersaulted helplessly off the mesa wall. Everything blurred except for the barrel of the rifle which crashed into his face. It split his lower lip, spraying blood over his chin and down on his shirt.

Somewhere toward the bottom of the mesa, Brannon jammed

the heel of his boot into the soft dirt and abruptly halted his fall. The jolt of the sudden stop sent a sharp pain up his left leg. When he pushed himself to his feet, the leg collapsed, and he slid another twenty feet down the mountain, crashing through several sagebrush and a cactus. Finally he lodged in a large sage. Blood oozed from gashes in his arms, face, neck. His right sleeve hung in shreds.

Struggling for breath, he rolled to his knees and gingerly stood, trying to keep weight off his left leg.

Somewhere up there is about a pound of my hide and a black hat shot full of holes. Shylock . . . they ought to call that mountain Shylock.

Shots ringing out from a couple hundred yards to the right started him limping toward the base of the trail. The two Porter gunmen who held down Fletcher and Howland were waiting for the others to work their way down the trail. As the sunlight faded, Brannon could only see their two shadowy silhouettes.

He was within twenty feet of the pair when one of them glanced back at him and exclaimed, "Good night, you're one of those new Carolina boys, ain't ya? What happened to your mouth?"

"It's Brannon," Brannon mumbled.

"Stuart Brannon—from Arizona? He's up there?"

"Yep," Brannon replied, "I seen him with my own eyes!"

"We got a gunslinger like Brannon pinned down!" the other man cheered between shots at Fletcher and Howland.

"Well, I'll be. We'll be the ones that finally lead down old Brannon! That'll make us famous!"

"We won't get to do it," Brannon drawled. "These two here you're shootin' at ain't nothin'. Brannon was up above them, and them boys ridin' down will get him first . . . unless . . . unless we just step back and let these two through. Then we'll close the gap on the next horse down. And bango, we'll have ourselves a gunslinger!"

"Stuart Brannon is really up there? We didn't see him go up the trail. Nobody new, 'cept you Matee boys."

"He's a tricky one."

"Let's do it. Let's let 'em by."

"What will Porter say?" the other argued.

"We gun down Brannon, and he'll probably give us a raise. Stuart Brannon . . . I still cain't believe it!"

"Back over in them rocks and let them through."

"Here they come. We could jist plug 'em from here."

"No, don't pull away from these rocks, boys. Brannon will be right behind, and he don't miss! You don't want to give that killer a chance to plug ya!"

"They got another horse with 'em?"

"That's my horse!" Brannon cried. "They cain't steal him! I'm goin' to get him, boys. You take care of things here!"

"Where's Brannon?"

"He should be the next man down. Watch out for him, boys. He's a killer."

Darkness covered the desert as Brannon hurriedly limped away from the guards and down the road to Magdalena. He hoped that somewhere ahead Fletcher and Howland had stopped to wait for him. But with El Viento riderless, he feared they might assume the worst.

Fierce gunfire erupted from back on the trail. Brannon wondered how long Porter's men would keep shooting at each other. As the pain in his leg increased, he slowed his pace. He was hobbling severely by the time he heard a shout from some bushes off the trail. Feeble light from the first stars gave the evening a dim light.

"I say, old man on the road, did you see anyone else coming behind you?"

"He's a Mexican," Howland cautioned. "He won't speak no English."

"If either one of you says, 'Good heavens, Brannon, you look frightful,' I'll bust every tooth in your head!"

Fletcher and Howland rode out from the brush with El Viento in tow. Howland lit a match and held it near Brannon's dark figure.

"My word, Brannon, what—"

"I don't want to talk about it."

"Mr. Brannon, you must've fought a dozen of 'em, hand to hand."

"Earl—"

"Stuart, did you get shot?"

"Look, I tumbled off that mesa, cracked myself in the lip with my rifle, and ripped my shirt and arms rolling into a sage." With great effort he pulled himself into the saddle.

"Where to now?" Howland asked.

"Magdalena. That city's so crowded they couldn't follow us through it."

"What's going on back there?"

"The ones at the bottom are shooting at the ones coming down."

"Why on earth would they do that?"

"'Cause I told them Stuart Brannon was on that mountain."

"What? They believed you?"

"For a minute anyway . . . let's punch these cayuses and get out of here."

The three rode hard for Magdalena, not stopping until they reached the center of the town. There they rested at the plaza, dimly lit by the faint wash of light from surrounding buildings. After the men had watered the horses and loosed the cinches, Brannon studied Howland.

"Earl, how's the leg?"

"It ain't serious as long as it don't get swollen."

"My word, Brannon, you're the hard case," Fletcher insisted. "Now precisely what happened back there?"

"Well, it started when El Viento ran off," he began, splashing water on his face. "And then—aah—!" he shrieked as the cold water hit the wounds on his face.

After catching his breath, he asked, "Earl, what happened to you last night?"

"We were in La Serpiente Dorada when Porter and about six of 'em entered. I guess he don't like Mexicans 'cause he made some remarks about me sitting at the same table with Miguel and Estaban. The next thing I know one of them is drawin'. Well, Miguel took a slug and everyone dove for cover. I downed that one, winged another, and hollered at Estaban to get Miguel out of there. Then I took a ricochet in the leg and busted a chair with the back of my head. When I came to, I was in a wagon with a couple drunks tied up next to me.

"Woolsey showed up about the time they was leavin' town. He was cussin' and hollerin' about the evils of Stuart Brannon, but it was dark and he didn't recognize me. Porter sent Woolsey on out with the herd, wherever that is.

"I figured they was goin' to shoot me, but then Porter said to stick me on a horse and take me up to the mesa 'cause I was fast with a gun, and he could use another hand. He stayed in town, but when he came ridin' in early this morning, he rounded up the men saying that Stuart Brannon was at a fiesta at Rancho Pacifica, and he figured the Señora had hired you to retrieve the cattle. That's why everyone was saddling up when you arrived. He wanted to get the cattle out on the desert as soon as possible.

"He tried real hard to convince me to ride along and tried to threaten me, but I told him in simple terms where he could spend eternity."

"So they were planning to ride out and get the cattle moving?"

"I think he might have sent Woolsey to get 'em going yesterday, and this bunch was to catch up with them. But now, with the Brannon around, who knows?"

"We'd better find Ramon before he gets caught between the herd and this new bunch coming in from the mesa," Fletcher urged.

"The first thing we have to do is take it real slow on these ponies all the way back to the hacienda and get new mounts.

Even El Viento can't take much more of this pace." Brannon saddled up and led the trio out of Magdalena.

A skyful of bright stars and a sliver of moon now offered a view of the desert as they rode east to the base of the mountains. The cool breeze of the night soothed Brannon's torn face. His cheeks and the back of his hands felt almost sunburned.

His thoughts caromed from outlaws.

To cattle.

To haciendas.

To señoritas.

To one special señora.

Lord, there's something different about her. All the others . . . all of them seem to be competing with Lisa. And none of them could ever measure up. But Victoria . . . she doesn't compete. She allows Lisa to be Lisa. She comes as her own person . . . she understands. It wouldn't break her heart for me to pull out the locket and glance at that picture. I wouldn't feel embarrassed to mention something that Lisa and I did.

Maybe it's the smile. Or the way she makes me laugh. Or the burden that we both carry. I enjoy being with her. 'Course, everyone enjoys being with her. But she doesn't know anything about me. And when she does . . . maybe I'm just kiddin' myself.

The slow trotting of the horses made the trip seem endless for Brannon.

Mile after mile.

Shadow after shadow.

Bounce after bounce.

His face burned.

His thoughts flitted about and then settled back to a señora in the yellow dress.

As the horses turned onto the three-mile drive that led up to the hacienda, Fletcher and Howland rode up beside him.

"Mr. Brannon, I've been a thinkin'. Do you believe me and Miss Julie should wait awhile and get our place settled in before we commence having children, or should we just get started right away?"

"What?"

"Well, Miss Julie wants to get right started with a family, and I think—"

"Earl, my opinion is that you won't have a whole lot to say in the matter. It seems like whenever a woman sets her mind to having children, there's no way to prevent it from happening. What in the world brought up this subject anyway?"

"I just got to ponderin' about the wedding and all, and the thoughts naturally turned to, you know, family matters."

"Well, I, for one," Fletcher interrupted, "envy you and Brannon."

"Envy?" Brannon slowed El Viento and gawked at Fletcher.

"Certainly. Here's Earl, engaged to a beautiful young lady, planning out his future. And on the other hand, here's Brannon who's decided to remain a monk all his life. It's my dratted indecisiveness that bothers me."

"I suppose you were thinking about a lady in Prescott?" Brannon joshed.

"Good heavens, yes. I've never run across a woman quite like her. All the charm and grace of a lady of the court and yet none of that pompous, insufferable snobbishness. My word, Brannon, you'll never realize what a prize she is."

"This is great, just great! We've got a dozen men somewhere behind us in the night who would love to shoot us full of lead and another dozen up ahead somewhere who are just as anxious. We also need to round up 850 head of cattle and drive them several hundred miles north . . . and you two are pining away like a couple of schoolboys."

"Well, it was a terribly long ride," Fletcher reasoned.

"Kind of dumb, isn't it?" Howland added. "Mr. Brannon, have you got some kind of plan to get the cattle back? I suppose you've been figurin' out every move."

"Yeah, well, I think we'll need . . . there's the *rancho*."

"We'll need what?" Fletcher quizzed.

"I'm thinking on it. It's just that my mind kind of . . . I was preoccupied. Anyway, let's get those new mounts."

"Brannon, by any chance were you thinking about a certain widow?"

Brannon didn't respond.

"She looked beautiful in that yellow dress, didn't she?"

"She understands, Edwin. You can't explain to just anyone the ache in your gut that won't go away after a loved one dies in your arms. But she understands."

"She makes you laugh," Fletcher replied. "A few days ago you told me you needed to find someone who made you laugh."

"Yeah, well . . . it just goes to show how tired we must be to let our minds carry on like that. Let's take it easy riding up to the gate. We don't want to draw any fire this time."

They walked their horses to the huge oak doorway that served as a gate to the grounds of the hacienda. A few bangs on the door brought footsteps running.

"*¿Quién es?*"

"It's Brannon! Is that you, Estaban?"

Slowly the heavy doors creaked open, and Estaban appeared holding a dim lantern.

"Ay, yi yi! Señor Brannon, what happened to you? Did you wrestle with a cougar?"

"It's a long story. Listen, we need to change horses. Do you have three solid mounts to lend us?"

"Certainly, Señor, I'll tell Martinez to change your horses."

"And I guess we'll need to change clothes and grab a bite to eat. You haven't heard from Ramon, have you?"

"No, Señor. I will get Maria to bring some food to the main room in the big house."

"We better eat out here," Brannon insisted. "No reason—"

"No, the ladies insisted that we wake them the minute you arrived. You are to meet them in the main room."

"How did the Señora know we would be coming in?"

"She is very wise. She understands much. Here, you take this lantern; I'll get another."

As the three sauntered toward the big house, Brannon could smell orange blossoms. The men opened the wide doors to the main room and let the night air drift in. He reached up to remove his hat . . . and remembered it was somewhere back on the mountain. Brannon stepped to the big fireplace, but it was cold and dark. He felt much too dirty to sit down on the leather furniture.

Pablo padded about the room lighting lanterns. Soon the room glowed.

"Now there's the Brannon *we're* familiar with!" Fletcher kidded. "I hope Señora Pacifica and Felicia don't frighten easily."

"I washed off at the fountain in Magdalena," Brannon protested.

"I would suggest that you dig through Don Rinaldo's trunk and find some new clothing."

"Remind me to dig some more cartridges out of our pack."

Just then Maria entered with a large platter of cold meat, cheese, and huge tortillas.

"*Ay, yi yi, El Brannon! ¿Qué pasó? ¿Qué pasó?*" Then she quickly disappeared in the shadows.

"Okay, I look bad. I'll go see what I can do." Before he left the room, Brannon grabbed a fist-sized wedge of cheese and stuffed it in his mouth.

Leather shoes scuffed across the red tile floor. Brannon turned to see lanterns swaying and two women walking into the main room. Earl Howland spoke first.

"Miss Reed?"

"My word, Harriet, what on earth are you doing here?" Fletcher choked.

"Msppt yedx frm," was all Brannon could mumble through the cheese.

"Mr. Howland, Mr. Fletcher, and . . ." Harriet walked over and stared at Brannon. "And I presume you're Stuart Brannon.

You know, you haven't changed a bit." She surveyed him up and down. "I would guess a herd of wild buffalo stampeded over the top of you."

"Harriet? Why aren't you in Prescott?"

"Felicia!" Victoria Pacifica called back down the hallway. "Bring your medicine box when you come."

"There's an emergency," Harriet explained. "As soon as I got the wire, I took the coach to Tucson and hired a driver to bring me here."

"What's the emergency? Is it about the land grant? Elizabeth? Is it from Elizabeth?"

Harriet Reed reached into the sleeve of her dress and pulled out a telegram. "Oh, no, it's not for you, Stuart. It's for Mr. Fletcher."

"Edwin?"

Fletcher took the telegram near a lantern to read it.

"What's it—" Brannon began to ask, but Harriet silenced him with an upheld hand.

"Good heavens, no! Oh, my word," Fletcher moaned. "Oh, dear lady . . . and I'm so far away."

Tears coursed down Edwin Fletcher's cheeks. "He was only sixty-one. Much too young. I should have . . . I mean, there was no way to know. But I should have been there!"

"Your father?"

"Heart attack. Just like that, in the lobby of the Foreign Office."

Brannon tenderly looked Fletcher in the eye and laid a hand on his shoulder. "I'm sorry, Edwin. Deeply sorry."

"We must hurry on with this cattle thing, I probably should—"

"You probably should get in the carriage with Miss Reed, drive straight to Tucson, and catch the train east. You've got to get home, Lord Fletcher."

"My word, it is finally true. Lord Fletcher. Well, I'm not walking away from my partner."

"You leave your money—and we're still partners. But you're going to board that train in Tucson. Right, Miss Reed?"

"Yes, I completely agree."

"Edwin, we've been through it all together, from Broken Arrow Crossing on, and you happen to be one of only two or three good friends I have left alive. So I'm telling you as a friend, get home. Cattle ranches come and go, but family . . . they're worth more than everything. Harriet, drag him over there and talk some sense into him."

Fletcher and Reed sat down on the leather couch and spoke in hushed tones. Felicia entered the room and set the box of medicines next to Brannon.

"No, no," he protested, "Earl needs the help first. See what you can do for his leg."

Felicia turned her attention to Howland while Señora Pacifica came to Brannon's side. "Stuart, what happened to you?"

"Well, we shot our way off the mesa with Porter's men, and I . . . I slipped and fell down the side of the mountain and landed in some brush."

"That accounts for the scratches and the dirt from head to toe, but what about all that blood?"

"Oh, yeah. Well, I sort of cracked my lower lip on my rifle as I tumbled down the hill."

"I presume that is the white shirt I gave you."

"Sorry, I'll be glad to replace it."

"Why?" She cracked a wide grin. "It's obviously not durable."

Felicia finished dressing Howland's wound and began working on Brannon. The white, sticky ointment felt cool to his face.

"Mr. Brannon, your face will be very puffy for a few days, but it should begin to heal. You seem to have a rash wherever you were scratched."

Victoria Pacifica brought food to a low table by the couch and offered some to the others. Fletcher stood and walked over to Brannon.

"Stuart, I'm afraid you and Harriet have convinced me. I really must go home for a while."

"I know. Look, Edwin, we both knew this day was coming."

"It's been quite an adventure riding down the trail with the legendary Stuart Brannon."

"If you say 'legendary' one more time, you'll never make it home, Fletcher." Brannon put his arm on his friend's shoulder. "You've got to come back and help me with spring branding."

"Oh, you'll see him before next spring," Harriet interjected. "Edwin promised that you would come up in the fall and escort me to England."

"England? You're going to England?"

"*We* are going to England. You and I, Mr. Brannon."

"But—"

"Edwin asked if our wedding could be at his family's country estate, and I said yes. You'll be the best man, of course, so you'll have a good reason to escort me."

"Wedding? England? You decided all of this in five minutes of talk? What about . . . I mean, you can't decide things that important so soon." His eyes searched the room. "Victoria, tell them."

She grinned. "From what I know, it sounds like a wonderful idea."

"Sure sounds swell to me," Howland chimed in, "but don't tell Miss Julie about a garden weddin' in England. No reason to give her more ideas!"

"Listen, Earl, I want you to pack up your gear and ride along with Fletcher and Reed back to Tucson. I think you ought to have that leg checked by a doctor."

"I ain't goin' to do it, Mr. Brannon."

"Look, I didn't ask if—"

"I'm sorry, Mr. Brannon, but I'm not quittin' this."

"It isn't quitting if I send you back."

"I appreciate your concern for my leg, but I'm seeing this through. I promised Miss Julie that I was going to bring home thirty cows and a bull . . . then we would get married."

"Well, certainly the deal still holds. You'll get the stock, it's just that—"

"No, sir, I'm staying right here."

"Earl, look, you don't—"

"Mr. Brannon, I made an agreement. And I'd live the rest of my life with deep regrets if I backed away now. Those thirty cows and that bull ain't a gift. I'm going to earn them. If I can't earn them, I don't deserve the likes of Miss Julie. That's all there is to it."

"Earl, you've got to be the most stubborn man on earth," Brannon fumed.

"The second most stubborn man on earth," Fletcher corrected. "Look, Earl walks like you, shoots like you, rides like you, punches cattle like you, fights like you . . . and now, the supreme compliment . . . thinks like you. Of all people, you should understand his viewpoint. It's exactly what a young Stuart Brannon would do."

Brannon ran his fingers through his grimy brown hair and sighed.

"It's just . . . everything's swimming around. Harriet's here in Mexico. Edwin's going home. Earl won't listen to reason. I don't know . . ."

Harriet came over and tugged at Brannon's dusty sleeve. "You will escort me to England, won't you?"

"Yes, yes, of course. Providing that I outlive Captain Porter's men, and bad water, and Apache arrows, and—"

"That would be frightfully slack of you, avoiding the wedding for a mere mortal wound," Fletcher teased. "I'll expect a better excuse than that."

"But things were about to settle down. It was going to be a peaceful rancher's life and—"

"Are we talking about the same Stuart Brannon?" Harriet Reed stepped back and stood next to Fletcher. "When has your life ever been peaceful and settled down? We love you, Stuart, just the way you are. I do believe you'd disappoint every one of us if you ever changed. We can't all be Stuart Brannon. We can't keep up your pace. Not even Earl. Things change, life goes on."

Victoria Pacifica stepped over to Brannon and entwined the fingers of her right hand into his left hand. He glanced down at her dark, tear-filled eyes.

She took a deep breath, then sighed. "But for some of us," she said softly, "life stands still for a very, very long time."

SEVEN

With two hours of sleep, a shave, and a clean shirt, Stuart Brannon left the Pacifica hacienda. Earl Howland rode beside him.

"Mr. Brannon, how many men do you figure we'll have to fight to get that herd back?"

"Well, Captain Porter didn't have more than eight to ten on the mesa . . . and some of them are wounded or maybe dead. He probably has about the same with the herd. So I figure twenty hands, tops."

"With Ramon, the others, and us, they still got us outnumbered pretty good."

"Yep. It will all depend on how many of them really want to fight. If the cowboys were all shanghaied like you, they just might not feel much loyalty to Porter. But, either way, I expect they won't lay down and give us the herd."

Brannon had no difficulty locating the trail of 850 head of cattle. Although a week old, the prints still were fairly clear.

He counted tracks of at least a dozen men. How many of those stayed with the herd, and how many ended up on the mesa, Brannon didn't know.

The trail crossed a wide creek bed, dry except for a tiny dribble of water. The riders had swung out into the desert to the south, then straight east into the foothills.

Going north along this lateral canyon, they must have looped out to see who might be following them. Then they cut back for the grass on the mountains . . . and up this valley because they wanted to head north. They've got to be expecting someone to follow . . . they'll have a couple of boys dropping back for scouts.

They ate what they could from their grub sacks, and Brannon found himself dozing off in the saddle of the short, blue roan he had borrowed from the hacienda. Estaban had called it the best cow pony on the ranch. It was a lively stallion with black mane and tail, and Brannon wasn't at all sure he would be able to cut cows with it.

Finally, about sundown, Howland rode up alongside.

"Mr. Brannon, we going to make camp here?"

"Earl, we'll just keep riding until we catch up."

"How will we find Ramon and his men in the dark?"

"Gunfire."

"You mean they'll already be shooting?"

"Yep."

"How do you know?"

"Ramon's got a lot of pride. He'll take those cows back on his own, if he thinks he can."

"He could get himself killed."

"So could we."

In the foothills they traced a creek up a side canyon to find clean water. There they ate a cold supper. While the horses grazed, Brannon flopped back on the grass and watched the evening twilight fade.

"Mr. Brannon," Howland quizzed, "don't you ever get nervous before a gunfight?"

"Nope."

"Aren't you afraid, just a tad?"

"Oh, sure I'm afraid. But I'm not nervous. I'm still in control of my senses . . . still able to think clearly . . . still able to do what needs to be done when the time comes."

"But you're afraid, too?"

"Sometimes more afraid than others. Depends on what you got to lose."

"What do you mean?"

"Well, I guess I wasn't too scared over in New Mexico or up in Colorado. I had no future and nothing worth holding on to."

"How about last year with the Collector's army at the ranch?"

"Well, I wasn't too scared then either because I knew I was right, and 'cause there was nothing else to live for if I lost the ranch."

"But you're scared now . . . I mean, a little scared?"

"Yep. And it's a definite weakness."

"What are you scared of?"

"The same thing you are, Earl."

"Well, I'm scared . . . you know, if I took a bad bullet . . . I'm scared that I wouldn't be around to marry Miss Julie, and we wouldn't be able to do all the things we've been plannin', and what a disappointment it would be to her."

Brannon nodded. "Yep. That's it. For the first time in a long while, I've got some things I don't want to miss out on."

"You mean getting the herd back and—"

"Nope. I mean being with Señora Pacifica."

"It makes a difference, don't it?"

"Yep."

Thoughts of a woman in a yellow dress gave way to longhorns and cattle rustlers. The men remounted and set out back down the trail before the first stars appeared. The night dragged on, long and silent. Neither man spoke much. They rode, walked, rested . . . rode, walked, rested. About daylight Brannon's mind turned again to Earl Howland's comments.

Lord, I would like to live through this one. I got a lot more talking to do with Victoria . . . and maybe even ask her to consider—

"Mr. Brannon, we've got visitors. Up on the right."

"Apaches. Don't raise your rifle, Earl, and keep riding slow. I see six on the crest of the hill. How many do you see?"

"That's it, but how many are on the other side of the hill?"

"That's a good question. Let's find out." Brannon turned his horse and began to ride up toward the Indians.

"What are you doing?" Howland protested, but followed close behind.

Brannon kept his horse at a steady walk, his hand cradling the Winchester on his lap and the warm breeze ruffling his hatless head. "Look, Earl, if we take off running, they'll figure we're scared. If we raise a gun, they'll figure we want a fight. If we walk straight at them, they just might think we're neither afraid nor want to fight."

"You ever tried this before?"

"Yep."

"Does it work?"

"Sometimes."

The six Apaches on horseback spread out on the top of the hill and waited for Brannon and Howland to approach.

"Mr. Brannon, look down there!"

As they reached the top of the hill, Brannon and Howland viewed other Apaches . . . men, women, and children . . . some mounted . . . one wagon . . . most walking in a loose line north.

"*Amigos, ¿hace habla Inglés?*" Brannon called.

"Do not come near our people," a spokesman replied.

"Where do the brave Apache go?"

"We return to our Chiricahua home."

"The blue soldiers will make you go back to White Mountain."

"We will not go there. We will go home."

"Who is your chief man?"

"Cholla is our war leader."

"Tell him I wish him well, but I fear for the lives of his people if he opposes the blue soldiers."

"Who shall we say gives such advice?"

"A friend of his grandsons, Filippe and Cerdo."

"And what name do you go by?"

"Stuart Brannon."

"The Brannon!" he shouted to the others.

Immediately the spokesman pointed his rifle in the air and fired a shot. Howland started to raise his gun.

"No, Earl!" shouted Brannon. "Wait!"

The Apaches below instantly stopped their journey and looked to the hill. Brannon saw another half-dozen riders galloping toward them.

"What's going on, Mr. Brannon?"

"They just want to go back home to Arizona. Don't point that gun unless I do."

"Yes, sir . . . but I'm a slight nervous."

Among the new arrivals was a gray-haired man wearing an unshirted vest. Brannon noticed scars on his neck and his right arm.

"This is the Brannon," the spokesman motioned to the newcomers.

The old man spoke in broken English. "What? He is not a giant? He is no bigger than you. Go and get Filippe and Cerdo. Brannon, we have fought before."

"Yes, I believe we have. Down along the San Pedro."

"And up in the mountains. You rode with General Crook."

"Yes, for a few months."

"The stories of your battles are told around our fires. Many say you must be part Apache."

"God in heaven assigns us to a people, and to be born an Apache was not a privilege he bestowed on me. But perhaps when I fight, there is some Apache in my heart."

The old man broke into a wide grin showing bright white, perfectly straight teeth in the midst of a very wrinkled face.

"Let us sit in the shade of the tree. I have too long been in the heat of the sun."

Cholla sat cross-legged with his back against the trunk of the tree. Brannon sat beside him on his left and Howland next to Brannon. The others sat across from them, except for the one keeping the horses. Everyone clutched his weapon.

"My grandsons have told us of all the kindness and protection you gave them on their journey. I am thankful for your concern."

At that moment a rider returned, and Filippe and Cerdo slid off the horse.

"El Brannon!" Cerdo cried. "You have come to see me?"

"Yes," Brannon added, "you and Filippe. When I saw the warriors on the hill, I thought I should ask about your health."

"You see, Grandfather? I told them . . . I told them all that El Brannon is our friend. And many did not believe."

"Where is your hat, El Brannon?" Cerdo asked.

Brannon glanced over at Howland and then back at the boy. "My hat is dead."

"Dead?"

"Yes, it was shot so many times that it died, and I had no time to buy another."

Cholla spoke quickly in Apache, and another rider rode down to the wagon.

"It would be a high honor among our people to kill the Brannon," the old man spoke slowly. Brannon kept his finger on the trigger of his rifle and looked for movement among the warriors.

None moved.

"But it is a greater honor to have the Brannon as a friend!" Cholla concluded with a smile. "The Brannon is a friend of Cholla and his grandsons. I will not attack your camp. Not here or in the land of your home. But others will not treat you so.

"The Great One, who assigns each man to a people, also assigns each people to a home. We must go home. To die in defense of one's home is a noble death. To die of starvation in a foreign land is the fate of cowards. Do you believe a home is worth fighting for, El Brannon?"

"Yes, I do."

"I still do not see the angels, Grandfather," Filippe complained.

"Only when in battle, little one," Cholla explained.

The warrior soon returned carrying a black object. He handed it to Cholla. It was a hat. Brannon eyed the black felt hat with the rounded crown.

"This hat was given to me by General Crook himself. The turquoise band was made by the Navajo. I stole it." He grinned. "And the eagle feather I pulled from the tail of an eagle with my own hands when I was much younger. Now I want you to have such a hat."

"It is a treasure beyond counting, my friend. I cannot take such a fine gift."

"You will take it . . . because it is a gift," the chief demanded. "And you will take it because it is two sizes too large for me, and it makes me look like a fool!"

Brannon accepted the gift, rolled the brim and creased the crown, and then placed it on his head.

"I thank my friend Cholla for the hat. Now I have a gift for Cholla." He reached into his boot and pulled out his knife, along with the sheath.

"This knife was pulled from my back at the battle of Apache Wells many years ago. It has never lost a battle since that day. The previous owner of this knife is the only one to count coup against Stuart Brannon."

The old man beamed as he took the knife and turned it over slowly in his hand. "The gift is much too generous."

"When we all get back to Arizona, Cholla and his grandsons are welcome to eat at the fire of my ranch."

"Yes, and in the mountains of our homeland, you will always be a guest among Cholla's people."

"Have you seen many head of cattle and many bad men with guns guarding them?"

"Yes, my scouts say they are now at the mouth of Palo Verde Canyon."

"Are there some Mexicans from Rancho Pacifica there as well? They are my friends."

"Yes, but there was a battle yesterday."

"Do I continue on the lower trail then?"

"That is not the quickest way. If you will ride over the mountain of rocks, you will be able to catch them more quickly."

"Is there a horse trail over the top?"

"There is an Apache horse trail. Perhaps only our people can so ride."

"Tell me, are the Mexicans pinned down?"

"Yes. They are in the ruins of the old ones."

"The Mogollon?"

"Yes."

"I must go to them now and help."

"There are two who guard the trail and many who shoot at your friends. Do you need help in your battle?"

"I will not include my friend Cholla in my battles. But someday we may fight side by side. No, there are some battles a person must fight by himself. However, there is one thing you can do. I would like to have from you two very old arrows. Perhaps ones not good for use anymore."

One of the men sitting across from Brannon jumped up, stepped to his horse, and retrieved two new arrows, handing them to him.

Brannon stepped to his horse and reached into the saddlebag for six rifle cartridges. He handed them to the warrior who gave him the arrows. "May each of these find as its target food for your family."

The man never smiled, but nodded acceptance.

"These arrows will help me. We must go now. May God look after and protect your people."

"And may the angels continue to watch after the Brannon."

Without another word the Apaches remounted and rode down the hill to their people.

"Nice hat," Howland said.

"Yeah, try not to shoot this one," Brannon sniped.

He and Howland remounted and headed toward the rocky mountainside.

"What was all that about the arrows?"

"They just might be our secret weapon."

"What?"

"Give me some time to figure it out."

Brannon discovered the Apache trail over the mountain of rock was a foot trail, used only occasionally for horses. He was relieved that the blue roan took well to the rock. El Viento would have had trouble.

The sun was on its way down when they began to descend the mountain. In the waning light they saw the herd of cattle several miles up the valley. The animals appeared to be in a canyon that followed a creek straight east. At the base of the canyon stood red rock cliffs, and scattered up the cliffs were various ruins of the Mogollon people. Somewhere in those ruins, only slightly visible to Brannon, he knew that Ramon and the others were trapped.

"Earl, those scouts are going to be right down there in those rocks."

"How do you know? I can't see them."

"'Cause that's where I'd be if I were them. Now I'd rather not have any gunfire and draw the others into it, but we have to face them first. So we'll leave the horses here. Then you sneak through those rocks until you're right at that point . . . see it?"

"Yep."

"When I bluff them back, you cut them off."

"But don't shoot them?"

"No gunfire . . . if possible."

"How you going to bluff them back?"

"A little Apache scare. Look! There they are." Brannon pointed as one hat, then another, emerged from behind the rocks.

Brannon took a good ten minutes to get a position in front of Porter's scouts. In one hand he carried his Winchester, and in the other the two Apache arrows. As he crouched among the rocks, he estimated he was no more than twenty feet from the men.

"This is about as boring as mud drying along the Mississippi," one of the men grumbled.

"Relax. They'll relieve us at supper time. At least we ain't gettin' shot at."

"I could shoot them Mexicans. They cain't hit nothin'."

"Yeah, that's what Woolsey thought, and he's dead."

"You watch the road for a while. I'm going to take a little siesta."

Brannon counted to five, let out a blood-curdling scream, and tossed the arrow as hard as he could in the direction of where he figured the man was standing.

"Apaches! Bill, there's Apaches!"

"Where are they? I cain't see 'em. Where are they? How many?"

Brannon let out another scream and tossed the second arrow high. It fell into the rocks behind the men.

"That's an Apache arrow! Maybe they're above us!"

"I'm goin' for help. You hold 'em off!"

"Hold 'em off? I cain't see 'em! You ain't goin' to leave me stranded!"

Suddenly both men went running down the road toward Porter's other gunmen.

Howland leaped in front of them and leveled his rifle.

"Hold up, boys," he ordered. "You're not goin' anywhere."

"Apaches! Run!" they screamed at him.

Then one of them seemed to recognize Howland. He started to raise his rifle, only to feel Brannon's Winchester crashing down on his head.

The second man swiveled his gun toward Brannon, and Howland leveled him with a blow to the head.

"Get a piece of rope, Earl."

"Where did you learn that scream?" he asked Brannon. "You almost had me believin'."

"Repetition. I've listened to it time and time again."

"Well, that takes care of the easy ones. How about those surrounding Ramon?"

"We'll need those arrows again." While Howland gathered the arrows, Brannon pulled an airtight of tomatoes from his grub sack.

"Earl, open this can. I forgot I gave my knife away."

Howland handed Brannon the arrows and opened the can of tomatoes.

"Now grab a handful of those tomatoes and mash them through the fingers of your left hand."

"What?"

"Like this." Brannon demonstrated as the pulp trickled through his fingers. He then snapped about six inches off one arrow and tossed the arrowhead and its useless shank to the ground. He placed the broken end between the fingers of his left hand and wrapped his bandanna tightly around the fingers so that it held the arrow in place.

He put his juice-stained hand to his chest.

"What does that look like?"

"Like you just been shot with an arrow . . . sort of," Howland replied.

"You do the same. We're going to ride right into them!"

"Soon as they reform along the road to fight Indians, we'll turn and jump them."

"Just the two of us?"

"Ramon and the others will come off the mountain and back us up."

"Ride right at them?"

"And even fire a few shots backwards at our alleged pursuers."

Spurring the blue roan to a gallop, Brannon and Howland fired several shots back at imaginary Indians and dashed right toward Porter's men.

Brannon screamed, "Apaches! Apaches! They gut-shot me, boys! Don't let 'em scalp me!" He rode clear past the startled men, then collapsed off his horse, and sprawled flat on the ground, clutching the arrow against his side.

Howland raced in behind, his body slumped in the saddle. One of the gunmen grabbed the reins of the horse. Howland slipped off the saddle and fell to the ground.

"Those are Apache arrows!" Porter shouted. "Get everyone away from the cliffs and guard that road from the south! I told you Apaches were on the prowl!"

Men dashed about shouting. Some dove behind rocks, and others mounted up and rode off. Brannon crawled toward the base of the cliffs.

"I don't see 'em. Do you see 'em?"

"Stay down! You never see 'em until it's too late!"

"I think I see one!"

Several shots were fired up the road.

Brannon stood and signaled for Ramon and the others to come down the mountain. With a wave of his hand he positioned them and Howland behind the gunmen. He fired a shot that sparked granite next to one of Porter's men.

"Throw them down, boys!" Brannon shouted.

One of the men turned to fire, but Mateo's shotgun silenced both the man and the crowd. Two of Porter's men spurred their horses wildly to the south.

"Let them go," Brannon hollered.

"There's Apaches comin'!" someone shouted.

"Nope!" Brannon called. "Just canned tomatoes! Now walk out in that roadway with your hands high. And pray that you don't have to scratch anything 'cause Mateo is awful quick on the trigger with that scattergun."

One by one, they came out.

"Jaime, take all their guns!"

"I knew that was you, Brannon," Ramon announced. "You had the blue roan. How is the hacienda?"

"Your sister is well. How many men does Porter have up there with the herd?"

"There are none with the herd."

"What?"

"There were eight men pushing the cattle. Two turned to fight as we rode up. They did not win."

"And the other six?"

"They turned toward Arizona and rode hard."

"The conscripts, no doubt. Then this is all of Porter's men?"

"Yes. They caught us off guard at daylight, and we took cover in the ruins."

"Where is Porter?"

"He didn't ride in with the others. Perhaps he, too, has fled to the border."

"Maybe . . ." Brannon paused. "But why—"

"*¡El Brannon! ¡Tenemos visitantes!*"

"Friends or enemies?"

"*¿Quién sabe? ¡Federales!*"

"Out here? Troops?" Ramon quickly mounted his horse and rode out to meet them.

Howland walked over to Brannon.

"Earl, hold my rifle while I try to wash the tomatoes off my hands."

"Ya know, Mr. Brannon, I really didn't think that would work. I mean, it did look sort of just like ya spilt your lunch or something."

"If people get scared enough, they see things different. Just like those shadows on the wall at night when you were a kid."

Brannon was shaking water off his hands when Ramon and two Mexican army officers rode up. They dismounted and walked toward Brannon. He offered his hand to shake and suddenly found one of the officers pointing a revolver at his head.

"What?" Brannon muttered.

"So, Captain Porter, we meet again. Arrest him, Lieutenant, and throw him in with those others."

"Porter? I'm not Porter!"

The officers turned to Howland who still held Brannon's rifle.

"Ah, El Brannon, we will take the prisoner now. I appreciate your help for apprehending this cattle thief."

"He's not Brannon! *I'm* Brannon! Earl, they think you're me."

"Oh, no, sir. That there is Mr. Brannon," Earl corrected.

"There will be a reward for your capture of Porter," the officer urged Howland.

"What did he say?" Earl asked.

"They want to give you a reward. Look, I'm Brannon!"

"A reward?"

"This impostor is trying to lie about his identity?" the Lieutenant probed.

"Ramon, tell him what's going on!"

"*Lieutenant, este hombre,*" Ramon said solemnly, pointing at Howland, "*es El Brannon.*"

"Ramon!"

"*¿Y este hombre?*"

"Porter."

"Ramon! You set me up and—"

"So you claim to be El Brannon?"

"I don't claim it," Brannon barked. "I am Stuart Brannon!"

"Very well, you will have a chance to prove it." The lieutenant handed back Brannon's rife, the barrel pointed toward the sky. "If you start to lower that barrel you will be shot. Now do the trick that Stuart Brannon is famous for."

"Trick . . . what trick?"

"The one where you can shoot so straight that you can fire a bullet directly up in the air and catch it in your teeth as it returns to the earth."

"What? You're mad."

"Are you going to do it?"

"Of course not!"

"El Brannon can catch the bullet. You therefore must be an imposter. Arrest him with the others."

"Ramon," Brannon growled as the officer shoved him toward Porter's men. "I'll tan your hide and tack it to the gate post!"

A wide grin broke over the lieutenant's face.

"Now, Brannon," Ramon said slowly, "we are even."

"I am sorry, Mr. Stuart Brannon." The lieutenant smiled. "I owed Ramon a favor."

Earl Howland turned his head and squinted his eyes. "It was all a joke?"

Brannon burst out in laughter. "So it's a day for charades? Let's start over. I'm Stuart Brannon."

"Yes, and I'm Lieutenant Castillo."

"Well, you will take these cattle thieves for us?"

"Certainly."

"Where will you be taking them?"

"From Hermosillo to Chihuahua."

"What about Porter . . . wherever he is?"

"We will have to pick him up next time. But I believe you have greatly reduced his numbers."

"There are two more tied up just down the road in the rocks."

"We will find them. May the rest of your journey go more peacefully."

"And yours as well."

Within fifteen minutes the Mexican troops had the prisoners bound and marching south.

"Ramon," Brannon chided. Then he started to chuckle. "Shoot the bullet up and catch it in my teeth? How did you invent such a story?"

"Many have heard it about El Brannon," he teased.

"Well, it's time to round up the cattle and drive them back to the hacienda. I want to count them, stick a road brand on them, and buy a remuda before we throw them out on the trail north. How many men do you have?"

"Counting you and Howland, there are eight of us."

"Ramon, you and Earl take a man and ride point. Lead us back to the hacienda. Mateo and Jaime will each take a man and spread out on the flanks. Me and this hombre will bring up the drags . . . keep 'em together and don't let them spread."

They drove cattle for several hours until sundown and then quieted the herd near a pool of water that would evaporate within a few weeks. Setting night guard, listening to the bellowing of the cows, and smelling meat cooking on the fire . . . For the first time since he could remember, Stuart Brannon was doing exactly what he had come to Mexico to do.

EIGHT

"Will you wear black today?"

"No, but neither will I wear bright colors. Es Domingo, I will wear the brown."

"Does this mean the days of mourning are over?"

"Felicia, the days of mourning for Don Rinaldo will never end. I shall carry his love for me and my love for him in my soul until I reach the gates of Heaven. But I do not have to wear black."

"Perhaps, Señora, but not all will understand."

"For them I will pray," Señora Pacifica responded.

For a few moments both women seemed content to hurry about the spacious room, completing their preparation. Victoria Pacifica stopped in front of a very large mirror. She straightened her belt . . . tugged at her sleeves . . . and brushed down the front of her dress. Then she glanced at her face. Lines forming at the eyes. A streak of gray foretelling the future. The neck no longer pencil thin. The chin beginning to surrender its firmness.

Don Rinaldo, you always will be a handsome, young vaquero. But the Señora . . . well, her youth will soon be forgotten.

She laced up her shoes and stepped across the tile toward the main room.

"Felicia, are you ready?"

"Yes, Señora. Shall we eat breakfast before going to the chapel?"

"Please, help yourself. I will have only an orange. Did Pablo leave last night or this morning?"

"This morning, I believe. He left fresh bread, some meat, and fruit."

"Is everyone gone?"

"Franco Grande is not feeling well and said he would be at his house if he was needed."

"And Estaban . . . what did he decide?"

"Señora, you know the answer. He is feeding the animals."

"It is always so quiet when everyone is gone. No children laughing. No shouts of joy."

"Or wails of despair."

"Yes, that too makes this home."

Carrying their food on a tray, Felicia and Señora Pacifica walked to a bench under the big oak in the middle of the yard and sat down. "Señora, you should not have allowed all of them to leave the hacienda with so much trouble all around."

"It is Domingo. All people deserve a day of rest and worship."

"But with the cattle thieves out there and Ramon and the others gone . . . perhaps some of the men should have stayed behind."

"I explained all of that to you yesterday. There are no cattle here to steal, and we will keep the gates bolted. We will ask God's protection, and we will accept His provision. To deprive people of their freedom to worship God is to cast them in the deepest of all dungeons. Besides, I enjoy the momentary stillness of the hacienda. It reminds me of happier times."

"Do you think about him often?"

"I suppose I never have him off my mind. You know, we met when I was only six years old."

"Mr. Brannon?"

"What? Mr. Brannon? No, no, I mean Don Rinaldo. Do you mean you were asking me if I think of Stuart Brannon?"

"Well . . . yes," Felicia replied. "You mentioned happier times, and I remember how much the two of you laughed the other night."

"You heard us laughing?"

"Yes . . . but I was trying to sleep."

"Did you hear us talking, too?"

"Yes, but I do not remember anything." Felicia blushed. "You were telling me about being six and meeting Don Rinaldo."

"I really must be more discreet in my conversations with Mr. Brannon."

"I am very sorry, Señora. Please go on."

"I was six years old. We lived at Monterrey in a very lovely home. And my father wanted to buy cattle to ship to Mexico City. Don Mecedo came to the city to make a deal with my father, and he brought his son, Rinaldo."

"How old was he at that time?"

"He was twelve."

"An older man?"

"Oh, yes, but he had never been to the city. I had to show him how to do everything. He could not walk two blocks without getting lost. You must remember those were the days when the streets of the city were safe. Not at all like today."

"He got lost?"

"More than once. I took him to the market, to the circus. He had never seen an elephant. Then one day we walked along the river, throwing rocks and making them skip. We came across two big boys who were beating a dog. It was a very ugly little dog, and they hit it with sticks as it cowered and tried to hide near a bench. It cried pitifully.

"Well, Rinaldo ran over to the boys and demanded that they quit. One boy said it was his dog, and he could beat it if he chose. Rinaldo pushed the boy back, and the little dog ran away. Then the boys said that perhaps they would beat him with the sticks instead.

"They were both much taller than he. One boy struck him with a stick, so Rinaldo knocked the boy to the ground and began to pound on him. Of course the other boy immediately began to kick Rinaldo viciously. One blow caught him above the eye, and he began to bleed."

"What did you do?"

"Oh, I was quite mature. I screamed and shouted for them to stop and then fell down and began to cry. I should have run for help, but I was too scared."

"What happened then?"

"They held him down and began to beat him until he stopped struggling. Then they rose to leave. Rinaldo jumped to his feet and started pounding on them. They could hardly believe that he would want the fight to continue. They were big boys . . . heavy boys, fat boys . . . and they began to tire. He would take all their punches and keep hitting back. Soon their faces, like Don Rinaldo's, were starting to bleed.

"One of them began to cry and ran away. Then the other one pulled loose and ran also. I looked up through my shameful tears as he came over to me. Besides the cut above his eye, his nose and his mouth were bleeding, and his shirt was torn. His leg was so bruised from the kicking that he limped. But when he got to me he said, 'Victoria, are you well? If they have hurt you, I will fight them some more.'"

She paused and looked away from Felicia, wiped her eyes, then took a deep breath and continued.

"I remember asking him, after we had washed his face in the river and were walking to my home, 'Why did you get into a fight over such an ugly dog?'

"'Because,' he said, 'what they were doing was wrong.' I looked at his swollen face. 'Why should you be the one to make the world right?,' I demanded. He answered, 'Why shouldn't I be?'

"That was the first day I loved Don Rinaldo. I went to bed praying that he would one day be my husband. We saw each other only once every year when his father came to sell the cattle. Every year we would walk and talk and visit the city.

"The year he became eighteen, he said he would not be back next year. He was going to Mexico City to serve in the army. He promised to return in four years. He said, 'I will come back on your wedding day.'

"I protested that I would surely not get married by then. 'Yes,' he said, 'you will marry on the day I return . . . and you will marry me.'"

"You didn't see him for four years?"

"Four years, two months, and ten days. I was sent to St. Louis to live with my aunt and study in an American school because my father hated the French rule. He felt that it would be better for all of Mexico to become part of the United States than to give in to the French. Anyway, we wrote as often as we could find someone to take a letter. And Don Rinaldo returned to Monterrey two months before I returned from school."

"After four years you were quite different, were you not?"

"Only on the outside. On the day I came home to Monterrey, we were married. The next morning we left for Rancho Pacifica. And this has been home ever since."

"It is a very romantic story."

"Marriage can be very romantic. But why am I telling you this? There's the chapel bell; it must be Estaban. Come, we must not be late."

The chapel at the hacienda was not a large building, but it was a favorite of Señora Pacifica. It was rectangular, about thirty feet long, and no more than twelve feet wide. Two lines of wooden benches were separated by a narrow center aisle. Every four feet, along the sides, where a window might be, stood a tall doorway with two narrow doors. In the warm weather the doors could all be opened to admit whatever breeze and aroma the hacienda allowed.

Señora Pacifica and Felicia were the only ones in the building when they retrieved hymnbooks on a table at the rear. They walked down the aisle and seated themselves in the front row, on the right, as always.

Señora Pacifica surveyed the front of the chapel. Pristine beneath a clean white cloth stood an oak table bearing a chalice and a loaf of bread. Behind the table was a narrow pulpit, silent in its authority, supporting a large, open Bible. In front of the table lay a polished oak kneeling bench, its leather cushions scuffed and wrinkled. The focal point of the room was the cross-shaped stained-glass window, imbedded high in the wall behind the pulpit.

Señora Pacifica would stop at the chapel daily to pray for the needs of those at the hacienda. And on rare occasions, a teacher or preacher would come down to speak at the tiny church. But most Sundays it had been just she, Felicia, Don Rinaldo, and one or two others. After her husband's death the Señora had begun to assume the responsibility of reading the Scripture texts.

Today she and Felicia read, sang a hymn, and then knelt for prayer. They repeated this procedure several times. A slight breeze blew through the open door, and the sun radiated a stained-glass blue across the table with the chalice. Finally Felicia arose and whispered that she would prepare lunch.

"Please, take something to Estaban and Franco Grande," the Señora instructed. "I will stay here for a few more moments."

With the room empty, she spoke aloud, though softly. "Don Rinaldo, this Brannon is a fine man. He will not let them beat the dog. We are very different in culture . . . but united in sorrow. He is a man of integrity in his prayers and, I believe, in his faith.

"If I could have anything in this world, it would be to have you back in my arms. But that will never be. I believe I would like to have Mr. Brannon as a friend. Not to take your place, but to help me when I need help. I think, perhaps, I might be of help to him also . . . "

"Señora! Señora! Come to the gate quickly! They are back!" Felicia called.

"The fiesta is over?"

"No, no! Not our people. Porter and a few of his men have returned!"

"Why? They took all the cattle last time."

"Come quickly. Estaban is talking to them!"

She raised her skirt above her ankles and scurried beneath the olive trees. The massive oak doors were bolted shut. Estaban stood on the right side of the gate, shouting through a narrow vertical gun slot in the thick adobe wall.

"Estaban, ¿quién es?"

"Son los bandidos . . . Les hablaré," he cautioned.

"I told you I want to speak to Brannon!" a voice shouted over the gate.

"Señor, I am very sorry; it is siesta time. I cannot disturb anyone at this time of the day."

"Then I will speak with the Señora!"

"I'm sorry," Estaban continued, "that is impossible. Perhaps you would like to leave a note?"

"A note? Do you realize who's out here?"

"Oh, yes, Señor. You are the one who steals cattle and shoots people."

"And I'm about to shoot you! Open the door, you stupid—"

"Franco Grande, ¡no! ¡No hora! Excuse me, Señor, I must ask you to stand back away from the gate when you speak that way."

"That's it, boys," Porter snarled. "Bust the door down."

"Señor," Estaban shouted, "please move back. Do you see the gun barrel, about belt-high, sticking through the adobe? I will wiggle it . . . see? And over on the other wall . . . *Franco Grande, meneo los cañones.* You see, these walls were built for defense. We are not very good shots, so we just put shotguns through those holes . . . then we pull the triggers at the same time. The barrels, as you can see, are aimed to hit everything standing within ten to fifteen feet of the gate. They tell me the cross-fire separates a man in half about at his belt. Of course, I have never seen it myself so it could be a slight exaggeration."

The men with Porter stepped back quickly.

"You're bluffing," Porter hollered.

"There is one way to find out. Send one of your men here to try and break down the door. Perhaps a skinny one would be less messy."

Porter backed away from the gate.

"Look, we don't want to shoot any of you folks. I just want Brannon to come out here. If he's not here, and I don't think he is, I must speak to the Señora. Now if you don't open, we'll have to climb over the wall and shoot our way in. Think about it. Do you want the women and children to get hurt?"

"Oh, no, Señor . . . please . . . if you are going to crawl over the wall, let me know so that I may first chain up the wolves."

"What wolves?"

"They are pets of the Señora, but they are very ungracious hosts, always hiding in the bushes or leaping from a building. They will not harm a flea . . . once they get to know you."

"You ain't got no wolves!"

"Franco Grande, permítanos oir su grito del lobo." Big Franco unleashed a howl that sent chills down the Señora's back.

"Brannon ain't there, is he?"

"Which Brannon do you wish to see?"

"There's only one! Look, I'm going to—"

"Captain Porter, there's folks coming up the road," one of the men announced.

Porter whirled and pointed his gun back down the long drive to the hacienda. The Señora stepped to the gun slot and peered out to see Tomas and his family walking behind the donkey cart, returning from Magdalena.

"Well, well, what have we here?" Porter exulted. "Sure looks like a nice family. I'd hate to see anything happen to them. Especially, the children!"

"Señora, ¿qué hacemos ahora?" Estaban asked.

"Pray, Estaban, pray."

"Mr. Porter, this is Señora Pacifica. Why are you threatening my friends?"

"Open the gates! Or some sweet little children will be orphans!" Porter's men surrounded Tomas and family. One of the girls began to cry.

"Mr. Porter," she demanded, "do not torment the children!"

"You're the one forcing me to it, Señora!" He grabbed a frightened Tomas by the front of his white cotton shirt. "Papa here gets the first bullet!"

"Wait! Do not harm them!"

"Estaban," she whispered, "take Felicia and Franco Grande and run through the chapel gate. Send them to Magdalena and let them warn the others to stay there. Then go find Brannon and Ramon."

"No, Señora . . . "

"Go quickly. Go with God. I am about to open the door."

"I cannot leave you."

"You cannot help me if you are dead. These men will kill you. I need you to find El Brannon."

"Señora, do you have your gun?" Estaban asked.

"Yes . . . with two bullets. One to save my honor, and one to send me to glory. You must find them quickly!"

By the time the Señora swung open the big front gates, the others were on their way out the concealed door at the back of the chapel. Porter's men burst through the gates, guns drawn.

"You three men go up the north side buildings, and you others take the south side . . . and watch out for them wolves," Porter commanded. "Me and the Señora will search the big house."

As he bellowed commands, Señora Pacifica waved off Tomas and his family, who quickly retreated down the drive.

Porter shoved her toward the big house. The Señora stumbled, then regained her balance.

I will walk proudly . . . and graciously. I will not lose my composure . . . Lord, help me . . . I will not cry.

"You got a fine place here, Señora. But you hacienda people are too stuck up. I've been around for almost sixteen years, and you ain't never asked me to your fiestas."

"I believe that is because you are a thief and a murderer," she replied without expression.

"Yeah, I know your type. We had 'em in the south too. Big old plantation houses. And slaves all over the place. But they wouldn't give me no mind. They treated them slaves better than me, and me a white man! That's all you are, a slave owner."

"I do not own these people. I pay them a salary, and they are free to move wherever they wish. They are my friends."

"Yeah, they're friends, all right. Where are they? Now let's just take a look at this place."

Porter grabbed the neck of her dress at the back and held his revolver close to her head. "If you got friends in these rooms, you better tell them to come out now. 'Cause if they startle me . . . I'm likely to pull this trigger."

"There is no one in this house." She measured each word so as not to sound nervous and at the same time slid her fingers under her wide belt and clutched the small, wood-handled pistol.

If he tears my dress . . . I will shoot him.

Roughly, Porter pushed her into each room and closet as he searched for others.

"This place is empty!" he growled.

"I told you that."

He threw her down in a leather chair. She smoothed the collar of her dress and tucked her hair back into place.

I will not cry . . . I will not compromise . . . I will not plead . . . Lord, have mercy on me!

One by one, Porter's men came back to the big house.

"Captain, they're all gone . . . everyone. Ain't no one here but the Señora."

"They can't all be in town. How about the men who were at the gate?"

"They ain't nowhere."

"The back gate. There must be a back gate."

"No sir, there's no way out. Unless they climbed over the wall."

"It doesn't matter. Gather up plenty of food and change horses. And saddle one for the Señora." Porter turned to her. "Which one are you riding?"

"El Viento, the tall, black gelding," she answered and then hesitated. "No, no . . . I forgot, he is lame. The copper dun mare will do."

"Get yourself some ink and a pen. You're writing Brannon a note. Tell him that I'm taking you to Adobe Wells, and he's to meet me there with the herd. I'll be there one day after he arrives. I'll trade you for the herd. If he fails, you'll pay the penalty."

"Brannon has the herd?"

"Yeah, he bushwacked my men."

"How do you know that?"

"'Cause Milford just ran a horse dead to get me the news."

Señora Pacifica sat down at the desk and wrote hurriedly. After a few seconds, Porter glanced over her shoulder and snatched the paper from beneath her hand. He tore it to shreds.

"Now write it in English!" he charged.

She finished the note, stood, and handed it to Porter. By now his men had the saddled horses under the oaks in front of the big house.

"Now pull off them lace-ups."

"I shall not."

"Look, Señora, you're going take them shoes off. I don't want you trying to run across the desert. Now if you don't take them off . . . I got a man or two who would be more than happy to help you."

She slumped down on the chair and began to loosen her laces.

Lord, is this where it should happen? I would rather die at my home than on a lonely desert.

She slipped off her boots and stockings and stood barefoot on the tile. Porter guided her to the horses.

"Milford, tack that note to the front gate. Then you and Bill hang back and take care of things proper."

"What are they going to do?" the Señora gasped.

"Why, they're just going to close up your place . . . that's all. Now climb up in the saddle. Look at that—isn't that nice? A sidesaddle! 'Course you won't need the reins 'cause we'll just tug you along. In fact, you won't need your hands at all."

He jerked her hands behind her back and tied them with rawhide before she had a chance to draw her handgun.

I should have shot him in the main room! Lord, it would be a good time for Stuart Brannon and the others to arrive!

Two men led the way. Porter and the Señora followed with a fourth man behind them. The final two still were in the big house.

Señora Pacifica glanced back to watch the two men exit the house as smoke began to rise from the north wing.

"No!" she cried helplessly. "No!"

The two caught up with the others.

"Ain't much to burn in there, Captain, what with that tile roof and floor and adobe walls. But beddin', furniture, and pretty dresses went up right fast!"

Señora Pacifica turned her distraught face away from the smoke and flames.

Lord, do not let it spread to the people's homes. Please, Lord . . . please!

A tear streaked her cheek. She straightened herself in the saddle, held her head high, and forced all expression from her face. She twisted her wrists, trying to loosen the bite of the rawhide thong.

Several times Porter and his henchmen stared back across the desert to view the flames at the hacienda.

Victoria Pacifica fixed her eyes straight ahead.

They rode at a steady pace straight into the eastern mountains. The first night they camped near the divide along a narrow creek. The Señora, still in her Sunday dress, was forced to build a fire and prepare a meal from the supplies the men had stolen from her kitchen.

The beautiful, immaculate Señora now looked like a disheveled peasant. Walking barefoot had dragged her dress in the dirt, causing the hem to fray. She tried her best to keep her hair well-pinned.

Porter loosened her hands only to let her cook and tend fire. Five times she had determined to pull the small pistol and kill Porter. Five times she had resisted the urge to do so.

Lord, a few days ago I might have done it. But now . . . what if Brannon is on his way? What if he trades the cattle for me? What if there are more days to sit and talk and laugh and dance? Not until it is over . . . only then . . . only then can I shoot.

She was given a blanket on which to sleep and was bound hand and foot. Her only victory was convincing them to tie her hands in front of her so that she might sleep more comfortably. This allowed her to keep her hand on the pistol grip all night.

The next morning she rinsed her feet in the stream and tried to wash her face. She cringed at her soiled dress and at the lack of soap to cleanse the stickiness from her hands. Without a comb or brush she finally had to leave her hair the way it was.

They traveled the crest all the second day. Porter frequently eyed the trail behind them. She was surprised that he knew the mountains so well. And she was surprised that they allowed her to ride unmolested. She was seldom the topic of their conversation.

Instead, the men talked of selling the cattle and what they would do with five thousand dollars each. There was no talk of the capture of Baja. But there was plenty of hushed dialogue about doing away with Stuart Brannon.

She did not know how much was serious and how much was exaggeration—meant to throw her off their real plans. But she could tell that Adobe Wells would be much more than an exchange of courtesies.

During the first two days, as she gathered firewood, she searched about for poisonous plants to grind into the men's food.

On the third day she cooked them a feast instead. The beef strips were fried with onions, peppers, and green olives. She rolled them in the last of the large tortillas they had stolen. She also managed a peach dumpling out of an airtight of peaches and some sugar and flour.

After they had stuffed themselves, the man they called Bill came over to tie her up.

"Señora, that was a mighty fine meal, but I got to tie you up."

She held forth her hands.

"I don't get it," he spoke softly. "We're treatin' you like dirt, and you fix us a feast."

"Bill, you will be judged for your behavior some day, and so will I. I will not be able to use your inhumanity as an excuse for mine."

"They cain't judge us if they don't catch us," he bragged.

"There is a higher judgment than the law of the land."

He paused and looked into her eyes.

"You mean," he glanced toward the sky, "the judgment of God Almighty?"

"Yes."

"I don't believe in all that religion stuff."

"You will one day," she demurred.

"Not me."

"Yes, Bill, you will believe. There comes a day when every person believes."

"When's that?"

"On Judgment Day. But of course it will be too late to make a stand then."

Bill turned and went back to the others. She heard him mutter as he walked, "Them Mexicans is sure superstitious."

It was the last conversation she had with any of them except Porter, who talked repeatedly of how poorly he had been treated in the South before the war and again in Mexico.

On the evening of their third day from the ranch, they reached the northern tip of the mountain chain and looked down across the desert floor at Adobe Wells. They slept that night in a mountainside clearing, and the next morning they worked their way down to the wells.

Most of the morning Señora Pacifica was bound and placed on the ground beside a sage near the wells. The men walked about the ruins trying to determine whether to be at the wells when Brannon approached or let him arrive first.

Movement in the sage next to her startled her, and she strained to see the source.

A snake! Oh Lord, no!

She reached slowly for her little gun as the four-foot long diamondback slithered toward her.

If I scream, it will strike for sure. If I shoot it . . . I have lost my weapon . . . my last resort. If I don't . . . "

She clamped her eyes shut and started to pray. She felt the rattler pull itself up across her lap. She thought she would faint. She strained but could not open her eyes. She tried not to breathe.

Lord, it's stopped in my lap! I'm going to faint. I'm going to cry . . . I can't stop . . . Lord, I can't stop . . . I can't shoot it on my lap.

For a split second she thought about pulling the gun to her own forehead and squeezing the trigger before the snake could sink its fangs into her.

Lord, I don't want to die. Not here . . . not now . . . not like this. Oh Lord, I'm going to die!

Then, like a dark cloud moving on, the thought passed, and she composed herself. She could feel the snake slither off her lap. She slowly counted to fifty and squinted her left eye. Seeing nothing, she opened her right. Still nothing.

She felt numb, save for the perspiration cascading down her face. But she had won.

Soon she and the men were riding back up into the mountains to the east.

NINE

S tuart Brannon wanted twenty-four horses and a chuck wagon. What he had were six tired ponies and a nearly empty grub sack.

But Brannon knew all of that would change soon. As soon as they made it back to the hacienda . . . as soon as he had purchased a remuda . . . as soon as the cattle were ready to drive to Arizona . . . as soon as he had said good-bye to the Señora . . . as soon as he had acquired some sleep.

They drove the cattle for one full day after the Mexican troops departed. The next morning they started up a low row of foothills, on the other side of which, Ramon had assured him, they would sight Rancho Pacifica.

Brannon and Howland rode point.

"Mr. Brannon, do you think Porter is out there somewhere, waiting to try to take this herd back?"

"Earl, I've been thinking about it. His conscripts have made a run for the border, and most of his hired guns are with the Mexican troops. He can't possibly have more than five or six men left. And they aren't cattlemen. Personally, I think Porter's a coward."

"If they can't drive the herd . . . there's no reason to risk their lives gettin' it?"

"That's what I'm thinking."

Howland pulled his hat down and swung out around a calf that had wandered too far into the brush. Then he rode back.

"Of course, they could try to scatter the herd just for spite."

"Yep. I was thinkin' that, too," Brannon said with a slow nod. "But my best bet is that Porter rode for the border. He's about exhausted his recruits around here. Now up in Arizona there's always some riffraff hanging around mining towns."

"Then he could come back after us with new men?"

"Maybe. But by then I expect we'll be in Arizona, and he won't try such a scheme up there. No, more than likely Porter will get shot trying to rob a bank somewhere and die claiming he never got a fair shake at life."

They worked both sides of the point, keeping the lead animals grazing in the right direction. About an hour later, Brannon rode up to Howland.

"Mr. Brannon, these seem to be fine-looking animals."

"I think we're buying some good stock, Earl. You got your thirty head picked out?"

Howland pushed his hat back and let it dangle by the stampede string. "Whatever you cut out for me will be fine, Mr. Brannon."

"Nope. The first thing about the cattle business is knowing how to select good stock. You pick out thirty head by the time we get to the hacienda. We'll brand a Flying H on each of them."

"Flyin' H? Yeah, that would make a good brand!"

"Earl, ride back there and relieve Ramon. Tell him to ride point a while. I want to make sure we're aiming at the right hacienda."

Within moments Ramon galloped up to Brannon.

"You might want to save the strength of your pony," Brannon cautioned. "We've worked these horses harder than we should have."

"Yes, but we are near the hacienda now."

"What direction?"

"Northwest, over that pass. We should be able to see it in the distance."

"How much farther?"

"About ten miles from here . . . seven from *el paso*."

Brannon and Ramon rode ahead of the herd and stopped at the pass to scan the valley floor. On the far side, closer to the mesas and the desert, lay Magdalena . . . just a dark green blot on the landscape.

Much closer to them, but still almost imperceptible, was a tiny blur of trees and adobe.

"Rancho Pacifica!" Ramon called out. "Perhaps one of us should ride on ahead?"

"I suppose so, but our horses are played out. It would be best to ease on down the mountain with the herd."

After cresting the pass, the cattle also seemed to sense home. They stopped grazing and began a slow trot toward the hacienda.

"El Brannon," Ramon called, "someone is riding out from the ranch."

Brannon looked at the horizon and watched a small, thin trail of dust drifting their way.

"Go on up and see who it is. And you might as well now ride on in."

Ramon spurred his tall, gray horse and flew off down the gently sloping mountainside. The figures were only two specks when they met, and a moment later Brannon saw Ramon gallop hard for the hacienda. The other rider raced toward the herd.

Brannon trotted down the slope to meet the rider whom he recognized immediately.

"Estaban, what is it?"

"It is bad . . . very bad. El Brannon, they have taken her, and I could not stop them!"

"Taken who?"

"La Señora! Porter and four men came to the ranch on

Domingo when all were at the fiesta. They kidnapped Señora Pacifica!"

"Kidnapped?"

"Yes, and they burned the hacienda."

"It's burnt to the ground?"

"Only the big house. The walls stand, but the roof collapsed and most of the inside is lost."

"How do you know it was Porter, Estaban?"

"I saw him with my eyes! Felicia, Franco Grande, and I were there."

"Why didn't you stop them! Why didn't you do something?"

"Oh, I tried, Señor. We held them back for a while, but when Tomas and his family came home from Magdalena, Porter threatened to shoot the children unless the Señora went with him."

"Why did he take her?"

"Because of you."

"Me?"

"Yes, he left a note that said you must drive the herd to Adobe Wells. There he will exchange La Señora for the whole herd."

"Adobe Wells? Drive them clear up there?"

"He said he would not arrive in Adobe Wells until after you get there."

"I don't believe it. No! Where did Ramon go?"

"To the hacienda. He could not believe my words either."

"Estaban, can you *vaquero*?"

"Yes, Señor."

"Then take point," he shouted and spurred the blue roan.

Lord ... no ... no ... no ... this can't be happening! Not now! Not the Señora! Lord, protect her! Protect her life. Protect her honor!

Long before he reached the outer walls of the grounds, he could see the remains of the big house in the middle of the hacienda. Most of the damage was in the Señora's side of the building. The roof still partially covered the main room, and the south wing appeared unscathed.

He galloped through the gates past the oak trees and jumped from his horse. He ran to the front of the house where Ramon was quizzing Felicia.

She was in tears.

"Did they harm her? Is she injured in any way?"

"El Brannon!" Felicia cried. She rose, threw her arms around Brannon and sobbed.

"We must go after her," Ramon demanded.

"Yes . . . yes," Brannon replied, still cradling Felicia. "Have the people take care of our horses. I will want El Viento, if he hasn't been stolen. Run the cattle on what is left of the grass on the north side of the hacienda and have someone prepare food for us. We'll need twenty extra horses to move the cattle."

"We cannot take the herd," Ramon protested. "It will slow us down."

"It's our only way of contacting them. If they don't see the cattle, they won't reveal themselves."

"But my sister!"

"I pray she will have God's wisdom and peace, Ramon. She is in His care now. They know they must keep her safe, or we will never trade away the cattle."

"Perhaps I should ride after the troops?"

"Even if you catch up with them, it would be too late. We have to take care of this ourselves," Brannon insisted. "We'll leave at daylight tomorrow."

"Tomorrow! It is my sister you insult!" Ramon stormed.

Felicia still clutched Brannon.

"Ramon, we can help Victoria best by getting this herd to Adobe Wells as quickly as possible. We will let them rest one night and then drive them for twenty-four straight hours. That way we can arrive at the wells before noon on the next day. There is no way we can get the cattle there any quicker."

Ramon began to give instructions to the people who had gathered. Each had a task, and each understood the urgency of the matter. Finally, Felicia released her grip on Brannon and sat down on the bench near an oak.

"Señor Brannon, please forgive my forwardness. My broken heart is no excuse for behaving so poorly."

"It's a good enough excuse for me, Felicia."

"You are very kind, Mr. Brannon, and you remind me very much of my . . . father."

"Tell me what happened, Felicia. Tell me everything that happened."

She did.

As she finished, Brannon sat down beside her.

"So Estaban has been scouting the mountains to find us?"

"Yes, he has taken it hardest of all. She forced him to leave the Rancho with me and Franco Grande. Estaban feels he has dishonored Don Rinaldo."

"To disobey the Señora would be the only dishonor. He did not do that."

"Perhaps . . . if El Brannon talked to him."

"I'll speak to him."

"Señor, are you a man of prayer?"

"It seems like I've been doing a lot of it lately."

"We are all praying for the Señora. Someone has been in the chapel ever since they took her."

"God will hear," Brannon encouraged her.

"Do you know how important she is to us, Mr. Brannon?"

"And she is important to me also."

"No, not in that way. Señora Pacifica is a friend to everyone who lives here. If any family runs out of food, she is the one who has plenty. If the babies get sick, she comes to the house and sits through the night with the parents. If there is a birthday, she supplies the piñata. If a man gets drunk and beats his wife, she forces him to stop or to leave.

"She makes sure we hear the sacred words of Scripture and teaches us the songs of Heaven. She tells us about the heritage and culture of our people. She reads us stories about life in the city. And she informs us about what is happening in the world.

"She listens to our heartaches and cries with our sorrows. She pushes her way into no one's home, but is joyfully welcomed in all.

"There is only one Señora Pacifica. We need her very much. She is our stability and our identity. We live better lives because of her love and example. Does this make sense?"

"Felicia, I understand. Maybe I understand all too well."

For the next two hours the air rang with the sound of busy, anxious people. Words were less gracious. Tempers were shorter. Petty annoyances loomed larger. Many grumbled because El Brannon had not yet gone after the abductors.

When all the residents of the hacienda gathered at the tables behind the main house to have supper, Brannon stood to address them. *"Mis amigos, no quiero que* . . . anyone to think that I am slow in rescuing the Señora. My desire is to reach her in the fastest possible time and then do all in my power to secure her safe release. We will trade this herd and a thousand more, if necessary, to see that she returns to the hacienda. I will not return to my home until she is safe among you, and her abductors face the just punishment for their actions.

"In such a pursuit, it is necessary to have strong men, strong horses, strong weapons, and a strong reason. We now have the reason and the weapons, but we must wait this one night so that the men and horses and cattle will be strong as well. To go more quickly would guarantee failure. And, I can assure you, I do not intend to fail!

"May God have mercy on Señora Pacifica. May God have mercy . . . *de todos nosotros!"*

Ramon spent most of the evening pacing from the bunkhouse to the barn to the main house . . . repeating the cycle again and again. After the evening meal, in the long shadows of twilight, family after family came up to Brannon and expounded their sorrow and fear over the Señora.

"She cares for us. In the city no one cares."

"She makes us laugh."

"She made us all feel important."

"She is lonely, Mr. Brannon. Since the death of Don Rinaldo, she is very lonely . . . but not as lonely as we are without her."

"We are simple people. We live a simple life. But Señora made us proud of our life."

"She is our angel."

Brannon's body rested most of the night, but he slept only a little. The scratches on his face were now only faint streaks, but the worry-lines about his eyes grew more intense.

Lord, I know Porter's type. He doesn't just want the herd; he wants to kill me. He'll use her to get even with me and kill us both if he can.

I still don't have this world figured out. A good, brave man like Don Rinaldo is gunned down coming out of his own chapel while some devil like Porter roams free. Lord, let me find her safe and well . . . let me bring her back to her people . . . let me bring her back to me! I'm really scared of losing her.

Brannon knew that to drive the herd so far and so fast would be a harsh strain on them, but this was not a time for worrying about fat cows. He and his men threw the whole herd out on the trail toward Adobe Wells and kept them moving in a narrow file. They allowed the herd to graze in the morning for a short time, and again in the evening. The rest of the time they moved. Brannon and Ramon led the herd. Howland rode the uphill flank. In all they were eight men.

After supper he allowed the men a two-hour rest. Then he called them all back to the saddle. Even though the moon was only a slim crescent, it offered adequate light, and Brannon's party was back on the trail before midnight.

After another rest just before daylight, Brannon and Howland rode ahead of the herd. They stopped near the last clump of oaks before the trail dropped toward the desert and the final march to Adobe Wells.

"Earl, once we get out in the desert they can watch our every move. They can sit at the water and wait . . . or they can perch up in those eastern hills."

"Which do you think they'll try?"

"I think they'll be in the hills. That way they can count the men . . . keep an eye on our movement."

"So what's our plan?"

"Our first concern is the Señora. We'll trade them straight across and plan on recapturing the herd on down the trail. But I really don't think that's the goal."

"They want to shoot ya, don't they?"

"Yep. What we need is a surprise . . ."

"How about that surprise?" Howland pointed to a caravan of travelers coming into view from the south.

"Cholla's people? They should be in Arizona by now."

"They must have rested up before taking on the desert. You figure they'll stop for water at Adobe Wells?"

"Without doubt . . . and you're right. They just might be the surprise we need."

"Will they fight for us?"

"I wouldn't ask them to. But they just might help."

Brannon rode El Viento out from the oaks on the west side where he would be visible to the Apaches, but not to anyone in the eastern mountains. Then he raised the barrel of his Winchester high in the air and circled it about his head. After several moments of doing this, he returned to the oaks.

"Did they see you?"

"Earl, if you can see an Indian, then he's already seen you first."

"Looks as if several are riding this way."

"Go back to the herd and hold them on that side of the mountain. I don't want Porter to stop us yet. Then you and Ramon ride back up here for a powwow."

Brannon was pleased to see Cholla, as well as two others, riding for the oak grove. By the time they arrived, Ramon and Howland also had joined him.

"My friend the Brannon wishes to see me? Why does he hide in the trees?"

"Cholla, we are trying to save Señora Pacifica. Captain Porter and his men have kidnapped her."

"I presume the men with the Señora are back in the eastern mountains." Cholla's deep voice spoke each word slowly.

"I need my friend Cholla's help to conceal my movements from the bad men."

"What help do you need?"

"I need to reach Adobe Wells without Porter knowing I am there."

"How can that happen?"

"I would like to disguise myself as one of your warriors and ride back with you now. Then I will trail with you to the well. When you are ready to leave, I will hide and stay behind."

"But they must have seen three of us ride to the grove . . . will they not be suspicious if four return?"

"I want your warrior to ride with the cattle. He can catch up with you later—I will give him a fine horse for his work."

"You do not look Apache." Cholla, as always, spoke without expression.

"We will trade clothing."

Cholla spoke in Apache to the two men who were riding with him. Both volunteered to trade with Brannon.

"Now, Earl, I have a very big job for you. I need you to wear my hat and ride El Viento."

"Why?"

"Because Porter will be looking for me. The risk is, he'll try to kill me first."

"And he will think that Earl is El Brannon," Ramon added.

"I can do it, Mr. Brannon." Earl grinned. "Maybe I'll have those angels watching after me now."

In moments Earl Howland was mounted on El Viento, wearing Brannon's bandanna and black felt hat with the eagle feather.

Brannon clothed himself in the simple shirt, pants, and sash of the Apache, and the warrior pulled on Brannon's chaps and Howland's vest and hat.

"You got plenty of cartridges, Mr. Brannon?"

"Yeah, enough to shoot them through about five times each."

"You don't look much like an Apache."

"He looks sick," Cholla grunted. "Like a worm under a rock that turns white." He scooped up dirt from around the oak trees, walked over, and rubbed it on Brannon's forehead and cheeks. "The reflection from the sun would blind us. Now you look more better."

Brannon mounted the Indian pony and carefully put his holster and revolver out of sight. He carried his Winchester across his shoulder as the warrior had. He stayed on the western side of Cholla and the other brave so as not to attract attention.

They caught up with the rest of the band just as the group entered Adobe Wells. It was easy for Brannon to dismount and stay out of the line of sight of the eastern mountains.

Filippe and Cerdo soon discovered him.

"You have become an Apache, El Brannon?"

"Only for a very short time, Filippe."

"You are a funny-looking Apache," Cerdo informed him with a snicker.

"There will be some shooting here soon, and I want to hide among the ruins."

"You hide from the shooting?"

"Oh, no. I will hide so that I might surprise them."

"Maybe we will stay and watch," Filippe suggested.

"No, you will go on with your grandfather."

"But I have not yet seen the angels!" Filippe complained.

"Well, the angels might be busy some other place today."

Filippe and Cerdo sat next to Brannon while they ate and rested. The women filled many containers with water. Brannon used the moments to review the layout of Adobe Wells.

If I were in Porter's shoes, I'd wait until the herd is strung out on the prairie. Then I'd move quickly to the Wells . . . wait until the cattle begin to smell the water. Once the cattle started running toward the water the cowboys would drop back and send the Señora out . . . no . . . that's only if he wanted the cattle. If he wants me, then he'll hold Victoria at gun point in clear sight. A trap . . . there'll be a trap. There has to be a trap. In clear sight . . . on the top of the boulders. If I could hide in the boulders perhaps.

"Filippe, the other day, when the mean man was shooting at you out in those rocks, how were you able to hide from the bullets?"

"Out in the rocks . . . there is a ditch."

"A ditch?"

"Yes. Out in the jagged rock. It makes a little ditch almost like a cave."

"How little?"

"Oh, it is easy for Cerdo and me to hide in, but not you, El Brannon."

"How about a woman? Could she find safety there?"

"Perhaps, if she lay flat."

Cholla signaled for the people to prepare to move on. The women soon had everything loaded and the throng was on its way. Brannon had decided to lie flat behind the only three-foot wall left in town. He could view the herd that way, though Porter's approach would be out of sight.

As the Indians left, Cerdo walked by.

"El Brannon, until we sit together at a campfire, good-bye."

"Good-bye, Cerdo. Where's Filippe?"

"Probably begging Grandfather to let us all stay and watch."

Brannon lay on the ground as they left. The hot sand warmed him through the light Apache clothing. He positioned his gun belt to make his revolver more accessible and cocked the Winchester.

They may come down quickly . . . or late . . . or not at all. Lord, make it quick!

The Apaches had just left the scene when he spotted Howland, riding El Viento and wearing his hat, starting the cattle off the mountain and down into the desert.

The sky was clear. The bright sun baked Brannon's hatless head. He felt sweat drip across the dirt that Cholla had smeared on his face. With his shirt he wiped the sweat from his eyebrows and waited for the sound of horses.

Howland and the others had driven the cattle only about a third of the way to the wells when he heard hoofbeats from the east. His body suddenly relaxed as he caught a glimpse of Señora Pacifica among the riders.

She's alive! Ragged, perhaps . . . but alive!

As he expected, they stopped at the front of the wells. One man stood close to the Señora and held a gun pointed at her side. Porter stood behind them, also facing the oncoming herd. The other men spread out in the rocks and adobe rubble. Brannon knew he could shoot either the man with the gun on the Señora . . . or Porter . . . but he would not have time to shoot them both.

Whoever's left will shoot Victoria.

With the herd still a good distance away, Porter began to yell. "Brannon!"

"Is that you, Porter?" Howland yelled back. "Send the Señora out, and we'll turn the cattle loose!"

"Brannon, there has been a change of plans!" Porter bellowed. "You have done such a magnificent job of driving the herd this far . . . I will have you drive them to Yuma!"

"I ain't taking them farther. Turn the Señora loose!"

"We are going to Yuma. If you want to see her alive, you will drive the herd there!"

"We're makin' our stand right here!" Howland yelled back

from under the shadows of Brannon's hat. "You'll die at Adobe Wells, Porter."

"Maybe . . . maybe not," he hollered. "But the Señora will surely die right on this rock!" He, the other man, and the Señora climbed up on the rocks. Again Porter stood behind the Señora.

Suddenly Brannon stood up from behind the short wall and shouted, *"Salte a las rocas, Victoria!"*

He had forgotten that he now looked Apache, but the reaction was as expected. The man at the Señora's side whirled and fired his gun wildly.

Brannon's blast from the Winchester lifted the man off the rocks and tumbled him into the sage beside the well. Porter whirled and dove for cover when he no longer had anyone in front of him. The Señora, as he had hoped, jumped out into the rocks where Filippe had said there was the ditch.

"Ponga su cabeza abajo, Señora."

The other four men fired at Brannon, who dove behind more broken adobe. One bullet ricocheted off the rocks, ripped through his loose-fitting shirt, and grazed across his side leaving a streak of blood.

"I thought them 'Paches left!" one of Porter's men shouted.

"How many is there?"

"I cain't tell."

"There's only one! Circle him, boys! Circle him!" Porter roared.

Brannon rolled several yards to the right and then waited for a shot to come from among the rocks. When it did, he rose up to take aim at the outlaw about to fire at Brannon's former position. But a shot from back in the herd brought the man down before Brannon squeezed the trigger.

Now Porter's men took cover in both directions as Howland and the others moved in slowly.

"Brannon! I'll kill her!"

"You kill the Señora and you are a dead man! Let her walk to us and I'll let you ride off!" Howland shouted.

Brannon kept creeping to the west along the volcanic rocks. He was hoping to find the shallow ditch that would lead to the Señora.

"You're lying, Brannon!"

"Have you ever heard of Stuart Brannon lying?" Howland continued.

Earl, don't promise him too much!

"All right, Brannon! I'll let her go. Go on, Señora; go to your lover!"

"*Señora, ¡no avancer! ¡No hable! ¡Solamente quiero hallarla! ¡Arrátrese al oeste si puede!*" Brannon yelled, but most of his words were drowned by another round of bullets.

Again he moved further west to a new position. He was now on the coarse lava rock that burned and scraped through his thin clothing.

"Captain Porter, let's run for the horses! It ain't worth it! We're caught between Apaches and Brannon!"

"We're not leavin' without the Señora!" Porter cried.

"Well, I am!"

Brannon saw one man break for the horses. Suddenly Porter's arm appeared above the rocks as he squeezed off a round, shooting his own man in the back.

Raising his Colt, Brannon fired two shots quickly, the first striking Porter's hand just above the wrist.

Bullets again rained down on Brannon's position, and he crawled further out on the lava rocks. His cover now was scant, and shots repeatedly came at him from behind one of the crumbled adobe walls.

He turned his eyes off Porter's position and watched for a chance to shoot at the man behind the wall. The next shot sent rock splinters flying near his head, and he buried his face against the rough lava. When he lifted his head, blood was trickling down into his left eye.

Brazenly the man behind the wall raised his head to catch sight of the damage he had caused. He caught Brannon's bullet instead.

"Bill! Bill!" Porter yelled. "I'm shot in my shooting hand. You got to help me, Bill!"

"Bill's dead, Captain; it's just you and me. Forget the woman; let's get out of here! I'll bring the horses around!"

"You won't leave me, will ya? Don't leave me with this Apache!"

"I ain't goin' to leave ya, Captain. Now you ain't goin' to shoot me in the back, are ya?"

Brannon watched Howland and the others take up positions surrounding Adobe Wells.

"I ain't going to shoot ya in the back. Get the horses!"

"You promise on old Jeb Stuart's grave that you won't shoot me?"

"You're going to leave me, ain't ya? Ya yellow dog, you're going to leave me!"

"I ain't leavin' ya!"

If we can wait it out, they'll shoot each other.

Suddenly he heard Señora Pacifica scream. Then from her hiding place came the pop-pop of two light-caliber shots.

TEN

Brannon fired three quick shots at Porter's position and lunged for what he supposed to be Filippe's ditch. A flurry of bullets crackled around him, and he flattened his back against the cruel volcanic rocks. He had not found the small trenchwork in the ancient lava flow, only a runty indention.

"*¡Señora!*" he screamed. "*¿Qué pasa?*"

"*¡Una serpiente! ¡Tiene que dispararle a una serpiente!*"

"*¿Tiene más balas?*"

"No."

Bullets, rocks, dust, and smoke were flying in all directions, and Brannon felt thoroughly helpless.

If I go to her, they'll kill me. If I lie here, they'll find her. Howland and the others can't help. If they move closer, they have no protection at all. If they shoot from there, they might ricochet and hit anyone. Lord . . . it is time for a miracle.

The shooting stopped. He lay perfectly still.

Maybe they've run out of bullets.

He rolled onto this stomach and began to crawl across the rocks. Several shots forced him back to his original position.

Maybe they haven't run out of bullets.

Again everyone stopped shooting. Brannon withstood the temptation to raise his head. Then he heard a scuffle. The Señora cried out. A man grunted. Then he heard Porter shout, "I've got her, Brannon! I'm ridin' out of here! Don't think I won't shoot her! I got nothin' to lose!"

"You ain't goin' nowhere!" Howland called back.

"I mean it, Brannon! You better call off that Apache, or the lady dies!"

"That Apache does what he wants!" Howland replied.

"Tell her good-bye 'cause she's dead!"

"Don't harm her!" Brannon shouted, revealing his position.

"Who said that?" Porter cried out.

"It's me, Brannon."

"Brannon's on that black horse—"

"I'm no Apache. Don't harm the lady, and we'll let you ride off."

"Are you really Brannon?"

"I'll do 'til the real one comes along."

"Listen," Porter shouted. "Me and Hank is going to go for the horses. If you raise up, Apache Brannon, Hank will lead you down. Now you out there on the horses! I'm going to ride out of here with the lady on my horse. The second you pull the trigger, I'll kill her. Do you hear me?"

"Earl!" Brannon hollered. "Let him make his move!"

"*¡Señor Brannon . . . ¡No puedo permitir que se lleve a mi hermana una vez mas!*" Ramon called.

"*¡La matará!*" Brannon yelled back. "*¡Debemos hacer algo rápidamente! Permita hacer un traslado. ¡No disparsen por equivocation!*"

"Hank, keep your gun on that Apache—or whoever he is!"

Brannon could not risk peering at Porter, but stayed low. The outlaw's bloody right hand was wrapped in a bandanna, but it still held a revolver while his left hand clamped the back collar of the Señora's dress. He positioned her as a shield between Howland and the others and then fired several quick rounds in Brannon's direction.

Ducking the spray of lead, Brannon lost sight of the action. When he finally regained position, everything went crazy. Porter mounted his horse by the well, grasping the Señora behind him in the saddle to ensure that no one could shoot him in the back. Realizing that Porter was leaving without him, Hank aimed his rifle toward Porter and the Señora, but was immediately gunned down by Ramon and the others.

Brannon rose to his feet, but he found the volcanic lava flow nearly impossible for walking. He stumbled and fell as he tried to run across it.

Then, without warning, Filippe appeared on the broad granite rock by the well. He lifted his bow and fired an arrow, puncturing Porter's left leg in the thick part of the thigh. The horse reared and the Señora tumbled off. She thudded against the rock and lay motionless.

Porter spurred the horse among a wave of bullets from Howland and fired wildly at Filippe. The boy plunged to the ground with a scream.

Brannon stumbled and fell again, gashing his arms and hands as he fought his way off the lava flow. By the time he reached the well, Ramon was at his sister's side.

Brannon shouted at Howland, "Give me that horse, Earl!"

Howland vaulted from the saddle, and Brannon hurled himself upon El Viento.

"Is she dead?" he yelled at Ramon.

"No, she is not shot!"

"Earl, take care of Filippe!" Brannon spurred El Viento after Porter.

The outlaw rode no more than two hundred yards beyond Adobe Wells and then dove from his horse behind a carefully piled stack of rocks. He began to shoot at Brannon. Without even a sagebrush to hide behind, Brannon reined up and dove for the desert sand. El Viento immediately drifted back toward Adobe Wells.

Porter shot wildly now. Brannon knew the man was running low on bullets, courage, and blood. Brannon waited and then began to move in cautiously.

"Brannon! I'm bleedin' to death. I surrender! Do you hear me!"

"I hear you. You can't surrender."

"I surrender! Brannon, look. Here are my guns!" Porter cried out. "Look, I've thrown 'em out on the desert."

"How about your sneak gun?"

"I don't have one."

Brannon chipped away at the pile of rocks with bullets from the Winchester.

"Brannon, look . . . my sneak gun. I surrender. I'm dying, Brannon! Pull this arrow out of me!"

Brannon moved in slowly until he could see Porter propped against the rocks, his mouth open, breathing hard.

"Give me some water, Brannon. You wouldn't deny a dying man a drink, would ya?"

Brannon pulled the canteen off Porter's horse that stood motionless nearby and tossed the container down at the wounded man.

"You've got a shattered wrist and a little arrow in your leg. They won't be the cause of your death." Brannon cocked the Winchester and laid it beside Porter's head.

Howland rode up, leading the wayward El Viento.

"You can't shoot me," Porter whimpered. "I'm unarmed. I surrendered. I demand a jury trial!"

"They don't have juries in Mexico for swine like you." Brannon shoved the barrel so hard against Porter's head that the man fell over on the sand.

"We ain't in Mexico. These rocks . . . they're the boundary. This is Arizona. You can't try me in Arizona for crimes committed in Mexico."

Brannon grabbed Porter by the boot and dragged him to the south side of the rock marker. "Now you're in Mexico."

"You can't do that; it's illegal! You got to get me to a doctor." Porter began to crawl to the U.S. side of the monument. "You can't shoot me. Stuart Brannon wouldn't shoot a man who's unarmed and dyin'."

"Well, maybe *I* can," Howland declared and raised his rifle.

"Wait, Earl. He's not worth the regret. How's the Señora?"

"She came to. I think she's all right."

Brannon yanked the canteen away from Porter and collected the weapons that had been discarded. Securing them all on Porter's horse, he gave the reins to Howland.

"Take his stuff back there to Adobe Wells."

"You cain't do that! That's stealin'!"

"You're in no position to tell me what I can and can't do. Besides, I'm not stealing anything, Porter. We're just holding them for your arrival."

"You ain't gettin' me back into Mexico."

"Suit yourself, but it's a long crawl to Tucson. Remember, there's a band of Apaches just over the draw, and you just shot one of their children."

"Pull that arrow out, Brannon. You got to do that for me!"

"It'll hurt."

"It's killing me already!"

Brannon placed one boot against Porter's hip and gripped the shaft of the arrow with both hands. A quick hard tug and a yelp from Porter, and the arrow was out.

So was Porter.

"He fainted?" Earl wondered.

"Yep. Lucky for him it was one of Filippe's little arrows. Just a sharp stick with no arrowhead."

Brannon dug through the saddlebags on the back of El Viento and extracted a ripped flour sack that he had used to wrap his spare revolver. He tied the sack around Porter's leg wound and then mounted El Viento.

"We going to just leave him?" Howland quizzed. "We could take him back into Mexico."

"We'll leave him here for now. He can't go very far, and we

need to check on the others. If he goes north, he dies in the desert. His only hope is to crawl back to the wells."

"And reenter Mexico alone?"

"Yep."

"But how do we know that's the border?"

"How do we know it's not?"

"You really think he'd crawl back?"

"Wouldn't you?" Brannon rode hard back to Adobe Wells.

Several of Ramon's men scratched out graves for the dead, while he, Howland, and two others attended to the Señora and Filippe.

"Señora," Brannon called as he dismounted, "did you break any bones?"

"I have a headache. It is this brave warrior who is injured most severely."

She sat in the dirt leaning against the rock. She had ripped a piece from her brown dress to hold against Filippe's wounds. Earl Howland dismounted and gave the boy some water.

Brannon glanced up at Ramon. "We need to tell his people."

"The Apache warrior wearing your chaps has ridden ahead to tell them."

"El Brannon," Filippe called weakly.

Brannon bent down by the boy. He looked pale.

"Filippe, I didn't know you were in the rocks. It was not a good place for even a brave boy to be."

"I wanted to see the fight."

Brannon was surprised there were no tears.

"You were a part of the fight."

"El Brannon Apache and Filippe Apache . . . we defeated them, didn't we?"

"Yep. We sure did."

"Filippe and El Brannon . . . we are brothers. We fight on the same side."

He breathed deep gulps and held out his hand. Brannon held

the boy's hand, noticing it was as dirty as his own. They each were silent for a few moments.

"When my people come . . . you will not tell them I was scared?"

"Are you scared?"

"Yes."

"Do you hurt real bad?" Brannon asked.

"Yes. Very bad . . . very bad. I was shot twice. Once in the stomach and once in the back. The one in the stomach hurts the most."

"You lie still . . . get some rest," Brannon said softly, trying to comfort the youth.

Lord, you've got to help little Filippe!

"Tell me about the angels," Filippe asked.

"I don't know much about angels, Filippe. Maybe we should ask Jesus to tell you about the angels. He knows all about them. Have you ever heard of Jesus?"

"Yes, I have read some of His book. The lady who taught us English . . . she taught us to read the black book."

After a short prayer, Brannon glanced down at Filippe.

"May I have some more water?" Brannon reached for the canteen, but when he put it to the boy's lips, Filippe did not respond.

"Filippe?" He lowered his ear to the boy's chest and listened for a heartbeat.

"Is he dead?" Señora Pacifica whispered.

"No, he must have passed out. He's lost a lot of blood . . . too much blood."

"It wasn't two bullets, was it?"

Brannon pulled off his Apache shirt and rolled it up, placing it under Filippe's head. "No, it was one bullet that ripped clear through." He walked over to El Viento and pulled his own shirt from the bedroll. He buttoned the cuffs as he returned to the Señora.

"He will die?"

"Oh, maybe in the city with a good doctor by his side, he could live. But not here."

"Why did he do that? Why did he try to save me?"

"He was caught up in the battle. If you are a born warrior, it's very hard to watch a battle closely and not take sides. He picked our side. Señora . . . were you harmed by these men . . . in any way? You look—"

"I look terrible, I know. Ramon has already told me."

"No, but you have been through rough treatment."

"Yes, they treated me harshly, but they did not take liberties with me."

"I'm glad. It would have made me angry enough to sin. Where did you get the gun to shoot the snake?"

"I have carried a small weapon since the day that Don Rinaldo was murdered."

"So you had two shots all the time they held you captive?"

"Yes."

"Weren't you tempted to shoot Porter?"

"Many times."

"And why didn't you?"

"Every time I thought about it, I found I couldn't do it. It is not an easy matter to kill someone. Even if the person is despicable. Do you find killing easy, Mr. Brannon?"

"Never. But most times I'm not given a chance to think about it."

"You killed Mr. Porter?"

"No . . . not yet."

"Did he get away?"

"No. I would say he's crawling across the desert, trying to reach Adobe Wells."

"Coming to us? Why?"

"He will be very thirsty."

"Will you give him a drink or kill him?" she asked.

"I don't know the answer to that yet."

"What do we do now?"

"We will wait for Filippe's people to return for him."

"And then?"

"Then we will get you home to your people. Many are extremely worried. I also thought about you often over the past several days."

"Yes, and I have thought about you as well, Mr. Brannon. What have you thought?"

"I think . . . we should figure a way to visit each other more often. I very much enjoy your company, Señora Pacifica. What were you thinking?"

"I was thinking it is time that I call you Stuart and you call me Victoria."

"Mr. Brannon," Howland shouted, "you were right! Here comes Porter!"

"Is he walking?"

"Sort of like draggin' along. Should I help him, or shoot him?"

"Neither."

Seeing the struggling Porter, Brannon walked over to him as the wounded man approached Adobe Wells.

"Brannon, get me some water," Porter whined.

Taking the canteen off Porter's horse he handed it to Porter, who took two large gulps before he spoke.

"Brannon, you're a disgrace to the South."

Brannon raised the butt of his rifle, intending to strike Porter across the head. But the Señora called out, "Stuart, the man sounds delirious."

Brannon left the canteen with Porter.

He gulped the water down, letting much of it drip to the equally parched desert floor.

"Earl, you and Ramon pack Porter out to those lava rocks . . . there's a good-sized trench out there. It should contain him. Make sure he hasn't got any weapons."

"You can't do this, Brannon!"

Spitting curses and threats, Porter was placed in the volcanic trench.

Brannon checked again on the unconscious Filippe. Then he
retrieved his hat from Earl, slumped on one of the broken adobe
walls, and stared north. The Señora came and sat beside him.

"Thinking about the Apaches?"

"No. I was thinking about Liddon Segelke and Delbert
Crowden."

"Who?"

"A couple of friends of mine. We grew up not seven miles
apart, and sometimes we'd go rabbit hunting and pretend we
were in the army, ridin' with Sam Houston. We were all fourteen
when the war broke out. We rode two days to Austin to volunteer to protect Texas. I was first in line, and they told me I was
too young, so Delbert and Liddon lied about their age. They
claimed they were sixteen, and the army took them in. So I went
home to raise beef . . . and they went to war."

"What happened?"

"Well, the army didn't keep them around to protect Texas like
they had promised. Instead they were sent to the front lines of
the war."

"Did they die?"

"Yeah. Delbert at Missionary Ridge and Liddon at Vicksburg.
They could ride . . . they could rope . . . they could shoot straight
. . . and they could laugh . . . man, could they laugh. They were
good ol' boys. I'm still proud to have been their friend. But they
died in the war—and some demon like Porter lives. It just doesn't
figure, does it?"

"Perhaps you are in too big a hurry, Stuart."

"What do you mean?"

"You want a world that is perfect, now, where everyone is as
self-disciplined as Stuart Brannon. Where people do only the correct things. Where honor and virtue and industry are always
rewarded. Where each person will receive just what he deserves.
We'll have a world like that someday. But it might be a long while
before the Lord returns."

"Not for Filippe."

"No . . . I believe that will be Filippe's people now."

Brannon looked up to see three warriors urging swift horses toward Adobe Wells. When they arrived, he spent several minutes explaining to Cholla what had happened.

"Cholla, Filippe is a very brave boy."

The old man tenderly stroked the young boy's soft cheeks.

"Perhaps it is better to die brave than to live in defeat."

Brannon and Howland rode out with their men and settled the herd toward the eastern mountains where there was still a little grass to eat. Ramon built a fire, and the Señora began to fix supper. They all waited for the main body of Apaches to return.

"Mr. Brannon, what are you going to do with Porter?"

"Send him to the Mexican authorities, I guess."

"Where will you find them?"

"Perhaps in Magdalena."

"We ought to hang him at the Wells," Howland insisted.

"There aren't any trees."

"We could shoot him."

"Earl, it takes one kind of a person to shoot a man when he's throwing lead your direction. It takes another kind altogether to shoot a man who's no threat to you at all."

Brannon left two men on guard with the herd and led the others back to Adobe Wells for supper. They arrived to find all of Cholla's people encamped for the night on the north side of the wells. The Señora and Ramon were quartered on the east side toward the herd.

"They took Filippe to their camp," she said.

"Was he still—"

"Alive?"

"Yes."

"Unconscious?"

"Yes. He is burning up with fever also. I have said many prayers for him. Will it be safe for us to stay here tonight?"

"Cholla is a friend. We'll be safe."

"How about the others? Do you know them also?"

Brannon paced in front of the campfire, watching the stars begin to fleck the desert sky and listening to the chants of the Apaches.

"I had Ramon take Porter some water and a little food," the Señora said softly.

"How are his wounds?"

"Ramon said he is weak . . . and frightened. He thinks you will turn him over to the Apaches . . . and he believes if he comes up out of the trench, they will attack him."

"He's right."

"Then you will turn him over to them?"

"No. He's right about what will happen if they find him there."

"Then you will give him up?"

"I don't know . . . I just don't know. There ought to be laws and lawmen and jails and judges and juries and gallows. But out here there's nothing. If I were here by myself, I would just ride off and let the desert eat him."

"That is a grand speech, Stuart, but a poor lie."

"In what way?"

"You wrestle now only with yourself and your belief in God's judgment and justice. If no one else on earth were here but you and Porter, you still would be wrestling."

He stared at her through the laughing lights of the robust campfire. He watched as she tried using her fingers for a comb to smooth her hair, dirty and unkempt after three days on the trail.

"You aren't the first woman to see through me so quickly."

"And you are not difficult to understand. With you it is never a battle of guns and bullets and arrows and money and land. It is always a battle of morals, of philosophy, of faith, isn't it? I once knew a man very much like that."

Brannon had just returned from his shift on night guard at the herd and settled down next to the embers of the fire. He heard the soft Apache drumbeat swell in intensity.

Ramon sat straight up, still sleepy. "What is happening? The drums!"

Brannon almost whispered his reply. "A change . . . it must be Filippe. Wake the others. We'd better watch and see what they do next."

"El Brannon!" cried a young voice. "El Brannon, come quickly. Grandfather needs you!"

Cerdo appeared in the sage behind Brannon. He jumped to his feet and followed the boy to Filippe who was lying limp in the arms of his grandfather. Most of the people had gathered at Cholla's fire. And most sat expressionless, as though caught in time waiting for something to happen.

The drums and chanting ceased when Brannon entered the circle. One glance at the boy and Brannon knew Filippe was dead. Brannon sat down, cross-legged, next to Cholla and looked in silence.

The old man stared at the coals in the fire rather than at his grandson's body. Studying the chief, Brannon could detect neither sadness nor joy, relief nor anger. He waited for Cholla to speak.

"Before Filippe died . . ." Cholla's words were deep and very, very slow. "Before he died, he said, 'Go and tell the Brannon it is all right now. I have seen the angels! I have seen the angels!'"

Brannon nodded approval, but said nothing.

They all sat still by the small fire.

Men with battle scars long forgotten.

Women with babies at their breasts.

Children sleepy with inactivity.

Dogs with fleas.

Wrinkled, toothless old women.

Cholla with Filippe still in his arms.

Cerdo grasping his small bow and arrows.

And Brannon.

No one spoke for a long, long time.

It was Cholla's role to break the silence.

"When an old man dies a slow death, he has many sorrows. He grieves that he will not see his loved ones any more. He pains that he will not know if they grow to be wise and brave or cowardly and foolish. That is why most of the old die with regrets.

"But with my Filippe . . . I have lived long enough to see that he died a brave warrior. In the history of our people, he will be known as a warrior who died in battle."

After a brief silence, Brannon spoke. "In the history of my people, Filippe will be known as the friend of Stuart Brannon and hero of Adobe Wells."

"Yes," the old man said nodding, "that is right. That is right. At daylight we will go into the hills to say good-bye to Filippe. And by sunset tomorrow, we will be back at Adobe Wells to pick up the evil man you have hidden in the lava rocks. My grandson is dead . . . that man belongs to us now. The Brannon knows that is our custom."

Brannon weighed his words carefully. All the people seemed to be waiting for his response. "And Cholla knows . . . it is not my custom. He should be turned over to the Federales."

"We will fight, even die, to satisfy revenge for Filippe. Will you fight to the death to save this evil man?"

Brannon stood to leave their camp.

"Only God knows whether I will fight, Cholla."

He returned to the campfire of the Señora and found all were awake, awaiting him.

Victoria Pacifica sat up with her blanket wrapped about her shoulders, with only her head exposed.

"Filippe?"

"He's dead."

"What happens now?"

"They will march up into the hills to perform their final ceremony for him . . . then they return to the Wells. They want Porter."

"They know he's out there?"

"Yep."

"What will they do to him?"

"I suppose torture him a while and then kill him."

"Are you going to let them do it?"

"I've been wondering the same thing all evening."

"Stuart, you believe in divine providence, don't you?"

"Yep."

"Well," she continued, "I believe it would be fitting for God to appoint a snake to bite Mr. Porter tonight. By morning there would be no decision left for anyone to make."

"Yeah, that would simplify things. But my life has never been simple. There will be no snake or lightning to strike him dead . . . nor will he die of those wounds. There is a battle left to be fought in the spirit and the mind, and I must be the one who fights it."

ELEVEN

Brannon came off night guard at daybreak and roused Earl Howland with a gentle shove of the boot.

"Earl!"

"Time to roll out, Mr. Brannon?"

"Time to move 'em out."

Howland sat straight up, letting his bedroll drop to his waist. "We're movin' the herd?"

"I think you should get them into Arizona as quickly as possible."

"Me? What about you, Mr. Brannon? Is Porter still in the rocks? Alive?"

"Alive and cussing. I want you to take Jaime, Mateo, and Ramon's *vaqueros* and push the herd north today. They've had time enough on the grass, and you can hit Creosote Springs by nightfall . . . remember that draw that still showed green grass?"

"Yes, sir, I can do it. But what's goin' to happen here?"

"I'm going to send Ramon and the Señora home. They're needed at the hacienda."

"And you, Porter, and the Apaches?"

"Jehovah Jireh."

"What?"

"The Lord will provide."

After a hasty breakfast, Howland and the *vaqueros* returned to the herd and began to move them north.

Brannon found Señora Victoria Pacifica more difficult to convince. "You are going to face the Apaches alone? What are you thinking?"

"Some things are better done alone."

"Such as what? Being a hero? Or dying?"

"Hopefully, neither." Brannon glanced down at the brown toes protruding from beneath her tattered dress. Then he turned to Ramon.

"You and your sister must go back to the hacienda. The people are very worried about her. You both will be needed to rebuild."

"I believe," the Señora huffed, "that I will stay at Adobe Wells and see the outcome of this conflict."

"You need to go. Felicia is beside herself. Estaban will be—"

"Stuart, I will stay here."

"Ramon," Brannon pleaded, "perhaps if you spoke—"

"The Señora does not listen to her little brother." Ramon smiled.

"This is not a game!" Brannon argued. "You have to leave, and that's that! Nothing is likely to happen here anyway. You will just waste time by staying."

"If you thought nothing is going to happen, you would not be sending us all away. No, Stuart. You are sending us away because you are not sure what you will do when Cholla and his people return. In your mind you cannot justify giving up even one as worthless as Porter. And you cannot rationalize risking your life for him either. I will stay."

"It's out of the question. Now pack up your things and I'll saddle your—"

"Mr. Stuart Brannon of Arizona," she declared, "if you were my husband, then I would, under strong protest, do as you command. However, you are not my husband." She paused as a slight grin brightened her face. "Not yet, anyway. I will do what I decide is necessary."

"Look, this is getting out of—"

"Ramon, Mr. Brannon is correct. The people at the hacienda need some encouragement. You must begin riding home immediately. Tell them that I am fine . . . for a barefoot, disheveled, dirty-faced Señora. I will be one day behind you."

"I will not leave you here with—"

"Ramon. God alone knows why I must stay. I am asking you to go and give leadership to the hacienda."

"This is crazy! You two are crazy! Sister, just mount your horse and ride away. Leave that *hombre malo* out there to defend himself with rocks. It is more than he deserves."

"Will you go?"

"How can I go? Shall I tell them I deserted my sister with a madman and a band of Apaches? What will I tell the people?"

Brannon studied the Señora. He wiped the back of his hand across his mouth.

"Tell them," he glanced at Ramon, "that she is with Stuart Brannon, and he will safely see her home."

"Do you mean that?" Ramon questioned.

Brannon simply stared back, his tired eyes void of expression.

"Yes . . . yes," Ramon muttered, shaking his head. "I will go . . . I will tell them."

He saddled up and then rode back to where Brannon and the Señora sat.

"I think that it would be best . . . ," he began. Both of them gazed up at him. "No, it is useless. *Vaya con Dios, Victoria.*"

"*Vaya con Dios, Ramon.* I will be only one day behind."

She stood and watched as Ramon trailed south through the desert. Brannon went to check the horses. Then he returned and quietly kicked with his boot at the coals of the breakfast fire. He and the Señora moved to a spot of morning shade near the well. They settled down, seated on the sun-hardened dirt with their backs against a broken adobe wall.

He nodded at her dusty feet. "I wish that old boy hadn't thrown away your shoes."

"I have been barefoot before. I will survive. Once, when I was just a girl, we lived in a cave for three months hiding from the French troops."

"You? You lived in a cave?"

"Yes. You did not think you knew everything about me, did you?"

"No, it's just that I figured—"

"That I had always lived in a large house with servants and beautiful statues?"

"Sort of."

"We do not know each other very well, do we?"

Brannon pulled his hat off and propped it on his knee. "Nope. We don't."

"Oh . . ." she blushed. "I owe you an apology. I am embarrassed that I blurted out those words about marriage. It was not appropriate, and you should not take offense at them."

He smiled and nodded his head. "It's all right. Truth is, the same thought crossed my mind a time or two in the past few days."

"Yes, I know."

"You know? You know what I'm thinking? You know what I will do?"

"You are not hard to read, Stuart. You show your emotion in your face, and your decisions are splendidly predictable."

He sat silently and considered her eyes.

"You are a very pretty girl," he said softly.

"I was a pretty girl," she corrected. "Now I am the Señora."

"I'm telling you what I see with my eyes," Brannon insisted. "I am not telling you what you see with your eyes."

Again there was silence.

"Victoria, what would you do if you were in my place?"

"With Porter?"

"Yes."

"I do not know. That is why I am staying. I cannot decide, and I am not the kind who lives easily with indecision."

A curse from among the rocks brought Brannon to his feet. "I'll go check on the prisoner."

"He will want water."

"I know."

The moment Porter saw Brannon he began to yell. "Brannon, you've got to help me out of here. I can't take more of this!"

Brannon handed him a canteen. "You won't be here much longer. The Apaches will be back in the afternoon."

"You're not going to turn me over to them? Shoot me for God's sake, but don't do that!"

"You were right yesterday, Porter. I can't shoot an unarmed man who is absolutely no threat to me. Personally, I don't think it will go a whole lot better with the Federales. They'll form a firing squad and shoot you."

"At least give me a weapon to defend myself!"

"Give you a gun? You'd shoot me and the Señora in the back. If I were you, I'd be piling up a good supply of rocks. Maybe you could hold them back for a few minutes."

"You don't really mean it . . ." Porter pleaded.

"Put yourself in my place, Porter."

Brannon left him the canteen and returned to the Señora. Settling down next to her, he watched the dust cloud on the northern horizon as the cattle were driven out of sight.

"Victoria, you have a magnificent ranch. You must come north and visit mine. It's not nearly so grand . . . but I believe it is the most beautiful land in Arizona."

"I will look forward to the visit."

"There are some people I'd like for you to meet. Perhaps you could come in June when the grass on the mountain is still green."

"Oh, I cannot come up in June, it is festival time in Magdalena. Company comes from Monterrey . . . I have so much to do."

"How about July? You could come around the fourth . . . they put on quite a show in Prescott on the fourth."

"I have promised Felicia that I would stay at the hacienda that week. She has a suitor, a second cousin of Don Rinaldo, coming to visit her from the coast. She insists that I interview him."

"Interview?"

"Yes. She refuses to marry anyone unless I approve."

"Well, I guess that leaves us August?"

Señora Pacifica reached over to put her hand on Brannon's.

"I was thinking that May would be a good time to come visit. It is all right if Felicia comes with me, is it not?"

"Oh . . . yeah. May is great. Eh, the place won't be quite fixed up. I mean, I've been thinking about painting it and putting in some fruit trees and—"

"Do you think you need to make improvements to impress me?"

"I don't?"

"Look at you," she insisted. "You haven't had a bath or a shave in a week. You're covered with dirt and dried blood. Your face looks as if it has been horse-whipped. And your clothing as if it had been laundered in dirt. Do you truly think I am the type that needs to be impressed by outward appearances?"

Brannon leaned his head back on the adobe and chuckled.

"Look at me? Look at you!" he chided. "With a cup in your hand you could pass for a beggar on a city street. I would guess your hair has never been so messed up and dirty in your entire life."

"It is the new casual look," she teased, as she pulled wayward strands of hair across her upper lip and feigned a mustache. "Perhaps," she giggled, "I shall be a matador!" Then she quickly stood to her feet. "Look, someone's coming!"

Brannon rose and lifted his Winchester. In the distant north a freight wagon, pulled by four oxen, slowly wended its way toward them.

"What's this, so far from anywhere?" Brannon asked.

"Looking for water?"

"There's water on the road to Magdalena."

They watched a long time before the wagon team and the bullwhacker who walked alongside of them halted by the well. A young boy shouldering a shotgun rode in the front of the canvas-covered wagon.

"Howdy, Mister." The freighter nodded to Brannon. "Howdy, ma'am." He tipped his hat at the Señora. "Say, is she Apache?"

Brannon tensed, but the Señora spoke first. "No, I am Señora Pacifica . . . but I'm afraid you caught me at a bad time."

"No offense, ma'am. I didn't want to get this far off the road after I heard old Cholla was back on the warpath. I've been jumpy for two days."

"Cholla is nearby," Brannon replied, "but he's not looking for trouble."

"That ain't the way they tell it up north. Anyway, as soon as my passenger gets off, I'm going back to the main road."

"Passenger?"

"Yeah, this fellow from Tucson. Insisted on going to Adobe Wells. Paid me good money. I tried to tell him there ain't nothin' here, but he insisted he had friends waitin'. You folks must know him."

"No, we're not expecting anyone," Brannon replied. "At least no one from Tucson."

"Wallace!" he called. "Kick that old boy. Tell him it's time to get his satchel and get off."

"Yes, sir," the boy replied. "Do you want me to unhook the team?"

"Nope, we'll water them where they stand, then leave. I ain't hanging around here two minutes longer than I have to. Too close to Injuns. No offense meant to you folks."

"Is that you, Mr. Brannon?" Brannon gave a startled blink at the man climbing out of the back of the wagon.

"Reynolds? Read Reynolds? I thought you were laid up."

"Yes, sir, I was. I made an excellent recovery, indeed."

"Well, Read, this is Señora Pacifica."

"What happened to you two?"

"I guess we've had a bit of trouble."

"No doubt Brannon once again proved victorious," Reynolds boasted.

"Read is an unusual name, Mr. Reynolds," the Señora commented.

"Brannon, boy, am I glad to see you," Reynolds enthused. He reached into his coat pocket and slipped out a small book, opened it, and pulled out a newspaper clipping.

"Listen to this. In the Tucson paper, no less. 'Mr. Stuart Brannon of Yavapai County, returning from a successful trip to Washington, D.C., foiled a holdup on the Southern Pacific railroad yesterday just forty-six miles southeast of this city.' Then it goes on and on about how you did it.

"But now listen to this. 'Mr. Brannon was assisted in his exploits by one of the passengers, a Mr. Red Reynolds, believed to be from North Carolina.'"

"Red?"

"They got my name wrong."

"North Carolina? I thought you were from South Carolina?"

"Well, Carolina is Carolina. That's close enough for me. Yes, sir, that's me, all right. I bought twelve copies of that paper, I did!"

"Read, what are you doing out here?"

"Coming to join the cause, of course. Did Captain Porter send you to meet me? Where's town? Where do we camp?"

Brannon laughed and shook his head.

"Read, I like you, so you listen carefully. This is Adobe Wells. There is nothing here but snakes . . . and a little water. There is no army of the South. Porter is a petty outlaw who has lost what few men he had. Your best bet is to get on that wagon and ride on out of here."

"What? I don't believe this! I've got the flyer. I've got it all written down right here . . ." He fumbled through the book.

"Read, Porter is down in a trench in that rock pile, hiding from the Apaches who intend to hang him by his heels over a hot fire and peel his hide off in one-inch strips. He's been shot in the arm with a Winchester and in the leg by an arrow."

"Who sh-shot him?" Reynolds stammered.

"I shot him in the arm, and a brave little Apache warrior shot him in the leg."

"But why?"

"Cattle rustling, murder, and kidnapping to start with . . . but we could go on."

Reynolds just gazed blankly at the rubble of Adobe Wells.

"Do you mean I rode all the way from Tucson in that dry-goods wagon for this? Nothing?"

"Afraid so." Brannon shrugged. Then he stared at the wagon. "What did you say was in there?"

"Ready-mades. Dresses, trousers, shirts, factory shoes, and things like that. Combs, brushes, mirrors for the Spanish ladies, you know . . . no offense, ma'am." He tipped his hat at Señora Pacifica.

Brannon quickly convinced the freighter to stay just long enough for the Señora to select a few items for herself. As she rummaged through the supplies, Brannon led Reynolds out among the rocks to Porter.

In a brief but heated conversation, Porter told Reynolds to shoot Brannon . . . or to toss him a gun. When Reynolds refused, Porter spewed a long diatribe about both men's origin and gave his opinion of their worth.

Reynolds climbed down from the rocks shaking his head.

"That's the great Captain Porter?"

"It takes a wise man to know when to quit."

"Like General Lee?"

"Yep."

"Well, I'll be. I jist didn't expect . . . say, are the Apaches really coming here?"

"They sure are."

"Well, if you don't mind," Reynolds gulped, "I think I'll go on with these boys to Magdalena."

"That would be a smart thing to do."

Brannon started walking to the other side of the freight wagon.

"Do not come around yet!" the Señora demanded.

Five minutes later permission was granted.

She was wearing the brightest green dress he had ever seen . . . almost turquoise . . . with black lace trim. Her hair was neatly pulled back with a jeweled comb. She wore new black lace-up shoes.

"How do I look? I could not find everything, of course, but I do feel much better."

Brannon grinned. "You make me feel like an old sagebrush next to a beautiful rose."

"Here, this is for you. He had a shirt of the same material as my dress. You will look good in this color."

"Thanks, Victoria, but I couldn't wear anything that bright. Besides, a man could get shot from four hundred yards away wearing a shirt like that."

"Oh, well, then I will not buy the dress. I do not want to get shot either."

"What? No . . . no . . . I didn't mean—"

"Will you wear the shirt?"

"Yeah," he sighed. "Give me the shirt."

The freighter turned his wagon around and signaled for Reynolds and Wallace to load up. He turned his attention to Brannon.

"Well, Mister," he said, "I don't know why you folks is waitin' for 'Paches. But good luck. What was your name?"

"Brannon. Stuart Brannon."

"Bannon, you say? Listen—"

"Brannon, not Bannon."

"Well, say, I once knew a Bannon over at Stockton when I was freightin' up in the mother lode in Californy. You related to those Bannons? No, I think it was Bancock. Anyway, are you related to them folks in Stockton?"

"Nope."

"Just curious. That old boy still owes me five cash dollars. If you're ever over that way and run across him, tell him I ain't forgot it neither." With that, he cracked the whip and the wagon lumbered westward out of Adobe Wells.

"Well, Mr. Bannon, you really impressed him."

"I can tell you one thing—you're the one who looks impressive."

"Thank you very much. This will do nicely until I get my . . . oh . . . they all burned, didn't they?"

"You'll need to do some shopping."

"Yes, I certainly will."

For the next two hours they sat in what shade they could find and talked about cattle, fiestas, politics, sourdough bread, gold mines, buffalo rifles, and mates who had died in their arms.

The sun was past halfway when Cholla's people appeared in the distance. Brannon went to saddle the three horses and brought them around to the well. He loaded up the gear on the third horse.

"Is that horse for Porter?"

"Yep. Are you ready for this?" Brannon asked.

"Yes. Have you decided what you will do?"

"Nope."

"Is it not a good time to decide?" she asked.

"Which would you rather carry, a rifle or a revolver?" he asked.

"I am more confident with a revolver."

He pulled out his spare revolver from the saddle bag, checked the chambers, and handed it to her.

"You've got five shots loaded. Do you want another cartridge?"

"No, I'm sure this will be enough. It takes me only two shots to kill a snake. Are you going to bring Porter out?"

"Nope. Not yet. Let's walk out and meet them. It will be better to keep them away from the rocks."

Brannon and the Señora walked the horses straight out to meet the approaching band of Apaches. Cholla rode in the lead, resting a rifle on his lap, with Cerdo seated behind him. When they halted, Cerdo slipped off the back of the horse and ran to Brannon's side.

"El Brannon, Filippe went to be with the angels."

"You might be right, son." He put his hand on Cerdo's shoulder. The boy stood beside Brannon and Señora Pacifica.

"The Brannon has a nice shirt!" Cholla greeted. "And your woman has a very nice dress."

"Thank you," Brannon replied.

"I could see it for two miles in the desert air," the old man asserted.

"Yeah . . . I know. " Brannon scowled at Señora Pacifica.

"We will take the man in the rocks now," Cholla announced.

Brannon lifted his hand off Cerdo and raised his Winchester to waist height.

"I think it would be better for your people to go to Arizona without the blood of an American on your knives. Word will spread to the reservation, and it will not go well for your people. Let me bring this man to justice."

Cerdo backed away from Brannon. The Señora held her revolver out in front of her.

"If you were going to take him away, why did you not do it before we returned?" Cholla asked.

"Because Brannon and Cholla are friends. I do not hide my actions from my friends."

"Yes, that is good. But you must understand, we would be ashamed to leave Filippe in Mexico unavenged. It would make our spirits sick."

"I understand that, but I, too, am controlled by regrets. His crime is in Mexico, and it is for that government to punish."

"What government punishes those who kill Apaches? But do not fear, even as we speak, your worry is being solved."

Brannon whirled to discover that Cerdo had not slipped back

to the other Apaches, but had gone behind him and worked his way across the rocks carrying his bow and arrow.

"Cerdo! No!" Brannon yelled.

"He is Apache; he will avenge his brother's death," Cholla announced.

Brannon, the Señora, and all the band of Indians scrambled to the edge of the rock. Cerdo already was standing over the trench.

"He is not here, Grandfather!" Cerdo shouted. "No, here he is—"

A hand suddenly reached out of the jagged rocks and jerked the boy down into the trench.

"Cerdo!" Brannon called.

"Brannon!" Porter yelled. "I've got a gun on this boy. You let me out, or I'll kill him too! You know I will!"

"Porter, let him go. You don't have a gun!"

Suddenly a wild shot ricocheted off the adobe near Brannon. Everyone jumped.

"What do you call that?" Porter bellowed.

"My gun!" the Señora moaned. "I had forgotten . . . I threw it among the rocks when I shot the snake! But where did he get bullets?"

"He probably had some in his belt."

Cholla signaled for his men to spread out around the lava flow.

Brannon yelled again. "Porter, you fool, these Apaches will never let you out . . . you know that."

"You've got to convince them, Brannon! You've got to talk to them!"

"We must act quickly," Cholla told Brannon.

"Yep, you're right." Then he turned back toward the rocks. "Porter, look, there is a gray horse right here. You leave the boy unharmed, and I won't shoot you."

"What about the Apaches?"

"I don't control their actions."

"I'm telling you right now, Brannon. One shot and the boy dies."

"Victoria, how many bullets does that gun hold?"

"Two. But he has shot one."

"Yes, but he can reload."

"I'm comin' out, Brannon!"

With great effort, Porter struggled to the top of the lava rocks, grasping Cerdo around the neck.

As a lithograph drawing on the cover of a dime novel, the scene might have been humorous—a big man trying to hide behind such a little boy. But now, to Brannon, it looked only pathetic.

Porter, weakened from his wound, started to stumble and loosened his grip on Cerdo. At that moment the Apache boy leaped back for the trench, and Porter raised the Señora's small handgun to shoot him.

Simultaneously three shots rang out in the desert.

All three struck Porter between the neck and the stomach. He slumped motionless to the rock.

Brannon, Cholla, and the Señora lowered their guns. She dropped the revolver to the dirt and rubbed her hands. Then she slipped her arm around Brannon and put her head on his chest.

"I didn't know I would do that," she spoke softly.

"There was nothing else we could do." Brannon put his hand lightly on the back of her hair.

Cerdo came crawling off the rocks.

"Are you unharmed?" Cholla asked him.

"Yes, but I did not get to avenge Filippe!"

"Maybe there will be no more need to avenge." Cholla looked at Brannon. "We will leave now. It is a very nice shirt."

Victoria Pacifica stepped back from Brannon and looked up at the Apache leader.

"Cholla," she said with a smile, "you have a very good eye for shirts."

"Yes, I do," he replied without expression.

Brannon slipped off his vest and pulled the turquoise shirt over his head. "Cholla, it is a present to you from Stuart Brannon. When you wear it, you will remember when we fought on the same side of the battle."

Suddenly the old man beamed. He cast aside his old shirt and pulled on the new one. "When I see it," he added, "I will remember the lady who has a very good eye for shirts."

Within moments the entire band had moved north up the trail. Brannon, still shirtless, dug a grave in the sand next to the others and then pulled Porter's body off the rocks and buried him.

The Señora stood alongside as he committed the body to the ground.

"What would you have done if Porter had not found my gun and made such a desperate move?"

"I suppose I would have fought."

"The Lord has given us lives with many difficult decisions. And in the next several days, I believe we may both face a particularly demanding one."

"I think the Señora's probably right."

"Mr. Brannon," she said smiling, "did I ever thank you properly for rescuing me from Porter and his men?"

"Oh . . . well, I, eh . . ."

She turned to him and slipped her hand behind his neck, pulling his head lower. She kissed him delicately on the lips. As she pulled away, he blinked and straightened up.

"I think," he grinned, "that maybe I should stick around. Just in case the Señora needs rescuing again." He returned to the horses and pulled on his old shirt.

"You did not like the shirt?"

"It made me nervous . . . as if everyone was looking at me," he explained as they each mounted up. "I don't like to attract attention."

"Stuart Brannon, you attract attention everywhere on earth you ever go. You just didn't like the shirt, did you?"

"Eh, actually . . . no, I hated it."

"You have absolutely no taste in clothes!" she scolded.

"That's what other women have told me."

"And," she probed as they trotted toward the south, "what else have other women told you?"

Somewhere during the next sixteen hours on the trail, he answered that question. And many more.

They had walked the horses for several miles when they reached the long drive that led to the Rancho Pacifica hacienda. It was almost 10:00 A.M. When they remounted, Brannon insisted that the Señora lead the way.

She checked the hand mirror and straightened her hair. Then she spread the skirt of the bright green dress over the withers and neck of the horse. The reins were held lightly in her folded hands on her lap. She sat with her back perfectly straight and rode unswerving toward the gate of the hacienda.

Before she came within a hundred yards, the gates were flung open and children ran to her, laughing and cheering.

"Señora! Señora! We missed you!"

"Señora! I lost my front tooth! See? See?"

"Señora! We will have a fiesta tonight, no?"

"Señora! You are the most beautiful lady in the world!"

Once inside the hacienda all fifty or so inhabitants crowded around the Señora. Brannon led the horses to the barn. He turned as he heard a woman's footsteps. He swung around to see Felicia hurrying to his side.

"Mr. Brannon, I thank you from the bottom of my heart for bringing her back safely! I had two very great fears."

"Two?"

"Yes, I feared that you would find her dead."

"And the other?"

"I feared that you would take her away with you."

Brannon stared for a moment at the anxiety in the girl's eyes.

"She is home now, Felicia. The Señora Pacifica has come home to stay."